Getting Started with Python Data Analysis

Learn to use powerful Python libraries for effective data processing and analysis

Phuong Vo.T.H

Martin Czygan

BIRMINGHAM - MUMBAI

Getting Started with Python Data Analysis

First published: October 2015

Production reference: 1231015

Published by Packt Publishing Ltd.
Livery Place
35 Livery Street
Birmingham B3 2PB, UK.

ISBN 978-1-78528-511-0

www.packtpub.com

Credits

Authors
Phuong Vo.T.H
Martin Czygan

Reviewers
Dong Chao
Hai Minh Nguyen
Kenneth Emeka Odoh

Commissioning Editor
Dipika Gaonkar

Acquisition Editor
Harsha Bharwani

Content Development Editor
Shweta Pant

Technical Editor
Naveenkumar Jain

Copy Editors
Ting Baker
Trishya Hajare

Project Coordinator
Sanjeet Rao

Proofreader
Safis Editing

Indexer
Priya Sane

Production Coordinator
Nitesh Thakur

Cover Work
Nitesh Thakur

About the Authors

Phuong Vo.T.H has a MSc degree in computer science, which is related to machine learning. After graduation, she continued to work in some companies as a data scientist. She has experience in analyzing users' behavior and building recommendation systems based on users' web histories. She loves to read machine learning and mathematics algorithm books, as well as data analysis articles.

Martin Czygan studied German literature and computer science in Leipzig, Germany. He has been working as a software engineer for more than 10 years. For the past eight years, he has been diving into Python, and is still enjoying it. In recent years, he has been helping clients to build data processing pipelines and search and analytics systems. His consultancy can be found at http://www.xvfz.net.

About the Reviewers

Dong Chao is both a machine learning hacker and a programmer. He's currently conduct research on some Natural Language Processing field (sentiment analysis on sequences data) with deep learning in Tsinghua University. Before that he worked in XiaoMi one year ago, which is one of the biggest mobile communication companies in the world. He also likes functional programming and has some experience in Haskell and OCaml.

Hai Minh Nguyen is currently a postdoctoral researcher at Rutgers University. He focuses on studying modified nucleic acid and designing Python interfaces for C++ and the Fortran library for Amber, a popular bimolecular simulation package. One of his notable achievements is the development of a `pytraj` program, a frontend of a C++ library that is designed to perform analysis of simulation data (`https://github.com/pytraj/pytraj`).

Kenneth Emeka Odoh presented a Python conference talk at Pycon, Finland, in 2012, where he spoke about Data Visualization in Django to a packed audience. He currently works as a graduate researcher at the University of Regina, Canada, in the field of visual analytics. He is a polyglot with experience in developing applications in C, C++, Python, and Java programming languages.

He has strong algorithmic and data mining skills. He is also a MOOC addict, as he spends time learning new courses about the latest technology.

Currently, he is a masters student in the Department of Computer Science, and will graduate in the fall of 2015. For more information, visit `https://ca.linkedin.com/in/kenluck2001`. He has written a few research papers in the field of visual analytics for a number of conferences and journals.

When Kenneth is not writing source code, you can find him singing at the Campion College chant choir.

www.PacktPub.com

Support files, eBooks, discount offers, and more

For support files and downloads related to your book, please visit www.PacktPub.com.

Did you know that Packt offers eBook versions of every book published, with PDF and ePub files available? You can upgrade to the eBook version at www.PacktPub.com and as a print book customer, you are entitled to a discount on the eBook copy. Get in touch with us at service@packtpub.com for more details.

At www.PacktPub.com, you can also read a collection of free technical articles, sign up for a range of free newsletters and receive exclusive discounts and offers on Packt books and eBooks.

https://www2.packtpub.com/books/subscription/packtlib

Do you need instant solutions to your IT questions? PacktLib is Packt's online digital book library. Here, you can search, access, and read Packt's entire library of books.

Why subscribe?

- Fully searchable across every book published by Packt
- Copy and paste, print, and bookmark content
- On demand and accessible via a web browser

Free access for Packt account holders

If you have an account with Packt at www.PacktPub.com, you can use this to access PacktLib today and view 9 entirely free books. Simply use your login credentials for immediate access.

Table of Contents

Preface

The world generates data at an increasing pace. Consumers, sensors, or scientific experiments emit data points every day. In finance, business, administration and the natural or social sciences, working with data can make up a significant part of the job. Being able to efficiently work with small or large datasets has become a valuable skill.

There are a variety of applications to work with data, from spreadsheet applications, which are widely deployed and used, to more specialized statistical packages for experienced users, which often support domain-specific extensions for experts.

Python started as a general purpose language. It has been used in industry for a long time, but it has been popular among researchers as well. Around ten years ago, in 2006, the first version of NumPy was released, which made Python a first class language for numerical computing and laid the foundation for a prospering development, which led to what we today call the PyData ecosystem: A growing set of high-performance libraries to be used in the sciences, finance, business or anywhere else you want to work efficiently with datasets.

In contrast to more specialized applications and environments, Python is not only about data analysis. The list of industrial-strength libraries for many general computing tasks is long, which makes working with data in Python even more compelling. Whether your data lives inside SQL or NoSQL databases or is out there on the Web and must be crawled or scraped first, the Python community has already developed packages for many of those tasks.

And the outlook seems bright. Working with bigger datasets is getting simpler and sharing research findings and creating interactive programming notebooks has never been easier. It is the perfect moment to learn about data analysis in Python. This book lets you get started with a few core libraries of the PyData ecosystem: Numpy, Pandas, and matplotlib. In addition, two NoSQL databases are introduced. The final chapter will take a quick tour through one of the most popular machine learning libraries in Python.

We hope you find Python a valuable tool for your everyday data work and that we can give you enough material to get productive in the data analysis space quickly.

What this book covers

Chapter 1, Introducing Data Analysis and Libraries, describes the typical steps involved in a data analysis task. In addition, a couple of existing data analysis software packages are described.

Chapter 2, NumPy Arrays and Vectorized Computation, dives right into the core of the PyData ecosystem by introducing the NumPy package for high-performance computing. The basic data structure is a typed multidimensional array which supports various functions, among them typical linear algebra tasks. The data structure and functions are explained along with examples.

Chapter 3, Data Analysis with Pandas, introduces a prominent and popular data analysis library for Python called Pandas. It is built on NumPy, but makes a lot of real-world tasks simpler. Pandas comes with its own core data structures, which are explained in detail.

Chapter 4, Data Visualizaiton, focuses on another important aspect of data analysis: the understanding of data through graphical representations. The Matplotlib library is introduced in this chapter. It is one of the most popular 2D plotting libraries for Python and it is well integrated with Pandas as well.

Chapter 5, Time Series, shows how to work with time-oriented data in Pandas. Date and time handling can quickly become a difficult, error-prone task when implemented from scratch. We show how Pandas can be of great help there, by looking in detail at some of the functions for date parsing and date sequence generation.

Chapter 6, Interacting with Databases, deals with some typical scenarios. Your data does not live in vacuum, and it might not always be available as CSV files either. MongoDB is a NoSQL database and Redis is a data structure server, although many people think of it as a key value store first. Both storage systems are introduced to help you interact with data from real-world systems.

Chapter 7, Data Analysis Application Examples, applies many of the things covered in the previous chapters to deepen your understanding of typical data analysis workflows. How do you clean, inspect, reshape, merge, or group data – these are the concerns in this chapter. The library of choice in the chapter will be Pandas again.

Chapter 8, Machine Learning Models with scikit-learn, would like to make you familiar with a popular machine learning package for Python. While it supports dozens of models, we only look at four models, two supervised and two unsupervised. Even if this is not mentioned explicitly, this chapter brings together a lot of the existing tools. Pandas is often used for machine learning data preparation and matplotlib is used to create plots to facilitate understanding.

What you need for this book

There are not too many requirements to get started. You will need a Python programming environment installed on your system. Under Linux and Mac OS X, Python is usually installed by default. Installation on Windows is supported by an excellent installer provided and maintained by the community.

This book uses a recent Python 2, but many examples will work with Python 3 as well.

The versions of the libraries used in this book are the following: NumPy 1.9.2, Pandas 0.16.2, matplotlib 1.4.3, tables 3.2.2, pymongo 3.0.3, redis 2.10.3, and scikit-learn 0.16.1. As these packages are all hosted on PyPI, the Python package index, they can be easily installed with pip. To install NumPy, you would write:

```
$ pip install numpy
```

If you are not using them already, we suggest you take a look at virtual environments for managing isolating Python environment on your computer. For Python 2, there are two packages of interest there: virtualenv and virtualenvwrapper. Since Python 3.3, there is a tool in the standard library called pyvenv (https://docs.python.org/3/library/venv.html), which serves the same purpose.

Most libraries will have an attribute for the version, so if you already have a library installed, you can quickly check its version:

```
>>> import redis
>>> redis.__version__
'2.10.3'
```

This works well for most libraries. A few, such as pymongo, use a different attribute (pymongo uses just version, without the underscores).

While all the examples can be run interactively in a Python shell, we recommend using IPython. IPython started as a more versatile Python shell, but has since evolved into a powerful tool for exploration and sharing. We used IPython 4.0.0 with Python 2.7.10. IPython is a great way to work interactively with Python, be it in the terminal or in the browser.

Who this book is for

We assume you have been exposed to programming and Python and you want to broaden your horizons and get to know some key libraries in the data analysis field. We think that people with different backgrounds can benefit from this book. If you work in business, finance, in research and development at a lab or university, or if your work contains any data processing or analysis steps and you want know what Python has to offer, then this book can be of help. If you want to get started with basic data processing tasks or time series, then you can find lot of hands-on knowledge in the examples of this book. The strength of this book is its breadth. While we cannot dive very deep into a single package – although we will use Pandas extensively - we hope that we can convey a bigger picture: how the different parts of the Python data ecosystem work and can work together to form one of the most innovative and engaging programming environments.

Conventions

In this book, you will find a number of styles of text that distinguish between different kinds of information. Here are some examples of these styles, and an explanation of their meaning.

Code words in text, database table names, folder names, filenames, file extensions, pathnames, dummy URLs, user input, and Twitter handles are shown as follows: "We can include other contexts through the use of the `include` directive."

A block of code is set as follows:

```
>>> import numpy as np
>>> np.random.randn()
```

When we wish to draw your attention to a particular part of a code block, the relevant lines or items are set in bold:

```
>>> import pandas as pd
```

Any command-line input or output is written as follows:

```
$ cat "data analysis" | wc -l
```

New terms and **important words** are shown in bold. Words that you see on the screen, in menus or dialog boxes for example, appear in the text like this: "clicking the **Next** button moves you to the next screen".

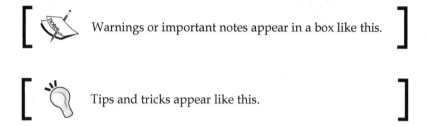

Warnings or important notes appear in a box like this.

Tips and tricks appear like this.

Reader feedback

Feedback from our readers is always welcome. Let us know what you think about this book—what you liked or may have disliked. Reader feedback is important for us to develop titles that you really get the most out of.

To send us general feedback, simply send an e-mail to feedback@packtpub.com, and mention the book title via the subject of your message.

If there is a topic that you have expertise in and you are interested in either writing or contributing to a book, see our author guide on www.packtpub.com/authors.

Customer support

Now that you are the proud owner of a Packt book, we have a number of things to help you to get the most from your purchase.

Downloading the example code

You can download the example code files for all Packt books you have purchased from your account at http://www.packtpub.com. If you purchased this book elsewhere, you can visit http://www.packtpub.com/support and register to have the files e-mailed directly to you.

Errata

Although we have taken every care to ensure the accuracy of our content, mistakes do happen. If you find a mistake in one of our books—maybe a mistake in the text or the code—we would be grateful if you would report this to us. By doing so, you can save other readers from frustration and help us improve subsequent versions of this book. If you find any errata, please report them by visiting http://www.packtpub.com/submit-errata, selecting your book, clicking on the **errata submission form** link, and entering the details of your errata. Once your errata are verified, your submission will be accepted and the errata will be uploaded on our website, or added to any list of existing errata, under the Errata section of that title. Any existing errata can be viewed by selecting your title from http://www.packtpub.com/support.

Piracy

Piracy of copyright material on the Internet is an ongoing problem across all media. At Packt, we take the protection of our copyright and licenses very seriously. If you come across any illegal copies of our works, in any form, on the Internet, please provide us with the location address or website name immediately so that we can pursue a remedy.

Please contact us at copyright@packtpub.com with a link to the suspected pirated material.

We appreciate your help in protecting our authors, and our ability to bring you valuable content.

Questions

You can contact us at questions@packtpub.com if you are having a problem with any aspect of the book, and we will do our best to address it.

1
Introducing Data Analysis and Libraries

Data is raw information that can exist in any form, usable or not. We can easily get data everywhere in our lives; for example, the price of gold on the day of writing was $ 1.158 per ounce. This does not have any meaning, except describing the price of gold. This also shows that data is useful based on context.

With the relational data connection, information appears and allows us to expand our knowledge beyond the range of our senses. When we possess gold price data gathered over time, one piece of information we might have is that the price has continuously risen from $1.152 to $1.158 over three days. This could be used by someone who tracks gold prices.

Knowledge helps people to create value in their lives and work. This value is based on information that is organized, synthesized, or summarized to enhance comprehension, awareness, or understanding. It represents a state or potential for action and decisions. When the price of gold continuously increases for three days, it will likely decrease on the next day; this is useful knowledge.

The following figure illustrates the steps from data to knowledge; we call this process, the data analysis process and we will introduce it in the next section:

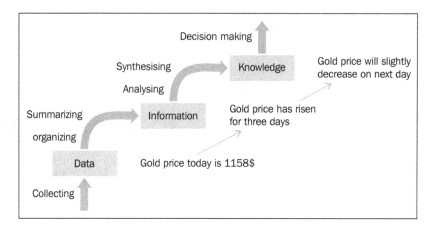

In this chapter, we will cover the following topics:

- Data analysis and process
- An overview of libraries in data analysis using different programming languages
- Common Python data analysis libraries

Data analysis and processing

Data is getting bigger and more diverse every day. Therefore, analyzing and processing data to advance human knowledge or to create value is a big challenge. To tackle these challenges, you will need domain knowledge and a variety of skills, drawing from areas such as computer science, **artificial intelligence** (**AI**) and **machine learning** (**ML**), statistics and mathematics, and knowledge domain, as shown in the following figure:

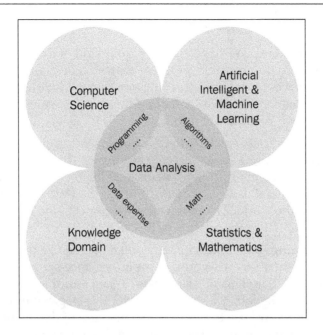

Let's go through data analysis and its domain knowledge:

- **Computer science**: We need this knowledge to provide abstractions for efficient data processing. Basic Python programming experience is required to follow the next chapters. We will introduce Python libraries used in data analysis.

- **Artificial intelligence and machine learning**: If computer science knowledge helps us to program data analysis tools, artificial intelligence and machine learning help us to model the data and learn from it in order to build smart products.

- **Statistics and mathematics**: We cannot extract useful information from raw data if we do not use statistical techniques or mathematical functions.

- **Knowledge domain**: Besides technology and general techniques, it is important to have an insight into the specific domain. What do the data fields mean? What data do we need to collect? Based on the expertise, we explore and analyze raw data by applying the above techniques, step by step.

Data analysis is a process composed of the following steps:

- **Data requirements**: We have to define what kind of data will be collected based on the requirements or problem analysis. For example, if we want to detect a user's behavior while reading news on the internet, we should be aware of visited article links, dates and times, article categories, and the time the user spends on different pages.

- **Data collection**: Data can be collected from a variety of sources: mobile, personal computer, camera, or recording devices. It may also be obtained in different ways: communication, events, and interactions between person and person, person and device, or device and device. Data appears whenever and wherever in the world. The problem is how we can find and gather it to solve our problem? This is the mission of this step.

- **Data processing**: Data that is initially obtained must be processed or organized for analysis. This process is performance-sensitive. How fast can we create, insert, update, or query data? When building a real product that has to process big data, we should consider this step carefully. What kind of database should we use to store data? What kind of data structure, such as analysis, statistics, or visualization, is suitable for our purposes?

- **Data cleaning**: After being processed and organized, the data may still contain duplicates or errors. Therefore, we need a cleaning step to reduce those situations and increase the quality of the results in the following steps. Common tasks include record matching, deduplication, and column segmentation. Depending on the type of data, we can apply several types of data cleaning. For example, a user's history of visits to a news website might contain a lot of duplicate rows, because the user might have refreshed certain pages many times. For our specific issue, these rows might not carry any meaning when we explore the user's behavior so we should remove them before saving it to our database. Another situation we may encounter is click fraud on news—someone just wants to improve their website ranking or sabotage awebsite. In this case, the data will not help us to explore a user's behavior. We can use thresholds to check whether a visit page event comes from a real person or from malicious software.

- **Exploratory data analysis**: Now, we can start to analyze data through a variety of techniques referred to as exploratory data analysis. We may detect additional problems in data cleaning or discover requests for further data. Therefore, these steps may be iterative and repeated throughout the whole data analysis process. Data visualization techniques are also used to examine the data in graphs or charts. Visualization often facilitates understanding of data sets, especially if they are large or high-dimensional.

- **Modelling and algorithms**: A lot of mathematical formulas and algorithms may be applied to detect or predict useful knowledge from the raw data. For example, we can use similarity measures to cluster users who have exhibited similar news-reading behavior and recommend articles of interest to them next time. Alternatively, we can detect users' genders based on their news reading behavior by applying classification models such as the **Support Vector Machine (SVM)** or linear regression. Depending on the problem, we may use different algorithms to get an acceptable result. It can take a lot of time to evaluate the accuracy of the algorithms and choose the best one to implement for a certain product.

- **Data product**: The goal of this step is to build data products that receive data input and generate output according to the problem requirements. We will apply computer science knowledge to implement our selected algorithms as well as manage the data storage.

An overview of the libraries in data analysis

There are numerous data analysis libraries that help us to process and analyze data. They use different programming languages, and have different advantages and disadvantages of solving various data analysis problems. Now, we will introduce some common libraries that may be useful for you. They should give you an overview of the libraries in the field. However, the rest of this book focuses on Python-based libraries.

Some of the libraries that use the Java language for data analysis are as follows:

- **Weka**: This is the library that I became familiar with the first time I learned about data analysis. It has a graphical user interface that allows you to run experiments on a small dataset. This is great if you want to get a feel for what is possible in the data processing space. However, if you build a complex product, I think it is not the best choice, because of its performance, sketchy API design, non-optimal algorithms, and little documentation (http://www.cs.waikato.ac.nz/ml/weka/).

- **Mallet**: This is another Java library that is used for statistical natural language processing, document classification, clustering, topic modeling, information extraction, and other machine-learning applications on text. There is an add-on package for Mallet, called GRMM, that contains support for inference in general, graphical models, and training of **Conditional random fields (CRF)** with arbitrary graphical structures. In my experience, the library performance and the algorithms are better than Weka. However, its only focus is on text-processing problems. The reference page is at `http://mallet.cs.umass.edu/`.

- **Mahout**: This is Apache's machine-learning framework built on top of Hadoop; its goal is to build a scalable machine-learning library. It looks promising, but comes with all the baggage and overheads of Hadoop. The homepage is at `http://mahout.apache.org/`.

- **Spark**: This is a relatively new Apache project, supposedly up to a hundred times faster than Hadoop. It is also a scalable library that consists of common machine-learning algorithms and utilities. Development can be done in Python as well as in any JVM language. The reference page is at `https://spark.apache.org/docs/1.5.0/mllib-guide.html`.

Here are a few libraries that are implemented in C++:

- **Vowpal Wabbit**: This library is a fast, out-of-core learning system sponsored by Microsoft Research and, previously, Yahoo! Research. It has been used to learn a tera-feature (1012) dataset on 1,000 nodes in one hour. More information can be found in the publication at `http://arxiv.org/abs/1110.4198`.

- **MultiBoost**: This package is a multiclass, multi label, and multitask classification boosting software implemented in C++. If you use this software, you should refer to the paper published in 2012 in the Journal*Machine Learning Research*, *MultiBoost: A Multi-purpose Boosting Package*, *D.Benbouzid, R. Busa-Fekete, N. Casagrande, F.-D. Collin*, and *B. Kégl*.

- **MLpack**: This is also a C++ machine-learning library, developed by the **Fundamental Algorithmic and Statistical Tools Laboratory (FASTLab)** at Georgia Tech. It focusses on scalability, speed, and ease-of-use, and was presented at the BigLearning workshop of NIPS 2011. Its homepage is at `http://www.mlpack.org/about.html`.

- **Caffe**: The last C++ library we want to mention is Caffe. This is a deep learning framework made with expression, speed, and modularity in mind. It is developed by the **Berkeley Vision and Learning Center (BVLC)** and community contributors. You can find more information about it at `http://caffe.berkeleyvision.org/`.

Other libraries for data processing and analysis are as follows:

- **Statsmodels**: This is a great Python library for statistical modeling and is mainly used for predictive and exploratory analysis.

- **Modular toolkit for data processing** (**MDP**): This is a collection of supervised and unsupervised learning algorithms and other data processing units that can be combined into data processing sequences and more complex feed-forward network architectures (`http://mdp-toolkit.sourceforge.net/index.html`).

- **Orange**: This is an open source data visualization and analysis for novices and experts. It is packed with features for data analysis and has add-ons for bioinformatics and text mining. It contains an implementation of self-organizing maps, which sets it apart from the other projects as well (`http://orange.biolab.si/`).

- **Mirador**: This is a tool for the visual exploration of complex datasets, supporting Mac and Windows. It enables users to discover correlation patterns and derive new hypotheses from data (`http://orange.biolab.si/`).

- **RapidMiner**: This is another GUI-based tool for data mining, machine learning, and predictive analysis (`https://rapidminer.com/`).

- **Theano**: This bridges the gap between Python and lower-level languages. Theano gives very significant performance gains, particularly for large matrix operations, and is, therefore, a good choice for deep learning models. However, it is not easy to debug because of the additional compilation layer.

- **Natural language processing toolkit** (**NLTK**): This is written in Python with very unique and salient features.

Here, I could not list all libraries for data analysis. However, I think the above libraries are enough to take a lot of your time to learn and build data analysis applications. I hope you will enjoy them after reading this book.

Python libraries in data analysis

Python is a multi-platform, general-purpose programming language that can run on Windows, Linux/Unix, and Mac OS X, and has been ported to Java and .NET virtual machines as well. It has a powerful standard library. In addition, it has many libraries for data analysis: Pylearn2, Hebel, Pybrain, Pattern, MontePython, and MILK. In this book, we will cover some common Python data analysis libraries such as Numpy, Pandas, Matplotlib, PyMongo, and scikit-learn. Now, to help you get started, I will briefly present an overview of each library for those who are less familiar with the scientific Python stack.

NumPy

One of the fundamental packages used for scientific computing in Python is Numpy. Among other things, it contains the following:

- A powerful N-dimensional array object
- Sophisticated (broadcasting) functions for performing array computations
- Tools for integrating C/C++ and Fortran code
- Useful linear algebra operations, Fourier transformations, and random number capabilities

Besides this, it can also be used as an efficient multidimensional container of generic data. Arbitrary data types can be defined and integrated with a wide variety of databases.

Pandas

Pandas is a Python package that supports rich data structures and functions for analyzing data, and is developed by the PyData Development Team. It is focused on the improvement of Python's data libraries. Pandas consists of the following things:

- A set of labeled array data structures; the primary of which are Series, DataFrame, and Panel
- Index objects enabling both simple axis indexing and multilevel/hierarchical axis indexing
- An intergraded group by engine for aggregating and transforming datasets
- Date range generation and custom date offsets
- Input/output tools that load and save data from flat files or PyTables/HDF5 format
- Optimal memory versions of the standard data structures
- Moving window statistics and static and moving window linear/panel regression

Due to these features, Pandas is an ideal tool for systems that need complex data structures or high-performance time series functions such as financial data analysis applications.

Matplotlib

Matplotlib is the single most used Python package for 2D-graphics. It provides both a very quick way to visualize data from Python and publication-quality figures in many formats: line plots, contour plots, scatter plots, and Basemap plots. It comes with a set of default settings, but allows customization of all kinds of properties. However, we can easily create our chart with the defaults of almost every property in Matplotlib.

PyMongo

MongoDB is a type of NoSQL database. It is highly scalable, robust, and perfect to work with JavaScript-based web applications, because we can store data as JSON documents and use flexible schemas.

PyMongo is a Python distribution containing tools for working with MongoDB. Many tools have also been written for working with PyMongo to add more features such as MongoKit, Humongolus, MongoAlchemy, and Ming.

The scikit-learn library

The scikit-learn is an open source machine-learning library using the Python programming language. It supports various machine learning models, such as classification, regression, and clustering algorithms, interoperated with the Python numerical and scientific libraries NumPy and SciPy. The latest scikit-learn version is 0.16.1, published in April 2015.

Summary

In this chapter, we presented three main points. Firstly, we figured out the relationship between raw data, information and knowledge. Due to its contribution to our lives, we continued to discuss an overview of data analysis and processing steps in the second section. Finally, we introduced a few common supported libraries that are useful for practical data analysis applications. Among those, in the next chapters, we will focus on Python libraries in data analysis.

Practice exercise

The following table describes users' rankings on Snow White movies:

UserID	Sex	Location	Ranking
A	Male	Philips	4
B	Male	VN	2
C	Male	Canada	1
D	Male	Canada	2
E	Female	VN	5
F	Female	NY	4

Exercise 1: What information can we find in this table? What kind of knowledge can we derive from it?

Exercise 2: Based on the data analysis process in this chapter, try to define the data requirements and analysis steps needed to predict whether user B likes Maleficent movies or not.

2
NumPy Arrays and Vectorized Computation

NumPy is the fundamental package supported for presenting and computing data with high performance in Python. It provides some interesting features as follows:

- Extension package to Python for multidimensional arrays (`ndarrays`), various derived objects (such as masked arrays), matrices providing vectorization operations, and broadcasting capabilities. Vectorization can significantly increase the performance of array computations by taking advantage of **Single Instruction Multiple Data** (**SIMD**) instruction sets in modern CPUs.

- Fast and convenient operations on arrays of data, including mathematical manipulation, basic statistical operations, sorting, selecting, linear algebra, random number generation, discrete Fourier transforms, and so on.

- Efficiency tools that are closer to hardware because of integrating C/C++/Fortran code.

NumPy is a good starting package for you to get familiar with arrays and array-oriented computing in data analysis. Also, it is the basic step to learn other, more effective tools such as Pandas, which we will see in the next chapter. We will be using NumPy version 1.9.1.

NumPy arrays

An array can be used to contain values of a data object in an experiment or simulation step, pixels of an image, or a signal recorded by a measurement device. For example, the latitude of the Eiffel Tower, Paris is 48.858598 and the longitude is 2.294495. It can be presented in a NumPy array object as p:

```
>>> import numpy as np
>>> p = np.array([48.858598, 2.294495])
>>> p
Output: array([48.858598, 2.294495])
```

This is a manual construction of an array using the `np.array` function. The standard convention to import NumPy is as follows:

```
>>> import numpy as np
```

You can, of course, put `from numpy import *` in your code to avoid having to write np. However, you should be careful with this habit because of the potential code conflicts (further information on code conventions can be found in the *Python Style Guide*, also known as **PEP8**, at `https://www.python.org/dev/peps/pep-0008/`).

There are two requirements of a NumPy array: a fixed size at creation and a uniform, fixed data type, with a fixed size in memory. The following functions help you to get information on the p matrix:

```
>>> p.ndim      # getting dimension of array p
1
>>> p.shape     # getting size of each array dimension
(2,)
>>> len(p)      # getting dimension length of array p
2
>>> p.dtype     # getting data type of array p
dtype('float64')
```

Data types

There are five basic numerical types including Booleans (`bool`), integers (`int`), unsigned integers (`uint`), floating point (`float`), and complex. They indicate how many bits are needed to represent elements of an array in memory. Besides that, NumPy also has some types, such as `intc` and `intp`, that have different bit sizes depending on the platform.

See the following table for a listing of NumPy's supported data types:

Type	Type code	Description	Range of value
bool		Boolean stored as a byte	True/False
intc		Similar to C int (int32 or int 64)	
intp		Integer used for indexing (same as C size_t)	
int8, uint8	i1, u1	Signed and unsigned 8-bit integer types	int8: (-128 to 127) uint8: (0 to 255)
int16, uint16	i2, u2	Signed and unsigned 16-bit integer types	int16: (-32768 to 32767) uint16: (0 to 65535)
int32, uint32	I4, u4	Signed and unsigned 32-bit integer types	int32: (-2147483648 to 2147483647 uint32: (0 to 4294967295)
int64, uinit64	i8, u8	Signed and unsigned 64-bit integer types	Int64: (-9223372036854775808 to 9223372036854775807) uint64: (0 to 18446744073709551615)
float16	f2	Half precision float: sign bit, 5 bits exponent, and 10b bits mantissa	
float32	f4 / f	Single precision float: sign bit, 8 bits exponent, and 23 bits mantissa	
float64	f8 / d	Double precision float: sign bit, 11 bits exponent, and 52 bits mantissa	
complex64, complex128, complex256	c8, c16, c32	Complex numbers represented by two 32-bit, 64-bit, and 128-bit floats	
object	0	Python object type	
string_	S	Fixed-length string type	Declare a string dtype with length 10, using S10
unicode_	U	Fixed-length Unicode type	Similar to string_ example, we have 'U10'

We can easily convert or cast an array from one `dtype` to another using the `astype` method:

```
>>> a = np.array([1, 2, 3, 4])
>>> a.dtype
dtype('int64')
>>> float_b = a.astype(np.float64)
>>> float_b.dtype
dtype('float64')
```

 The `astype` function will create a new array with a copy of data from an old array, even though the new `dtype` is similar to the old one.

Array creation

There are various functions provided to create an array object. They are very useful for us to create and store data in a multidimensional array in different situations.

Now, in the following table we will summarize some of NumPy's common functions and their use by examples for array creation:

Function	Description	Example

empty, empty_like	Create a new array of the given shape and type, without initializing elements	`>>> np.empty([3,2], dtype=np.float64)`
		`array([[0., 0.], [0., 0.], [0., 0.]])`
		`>>> a = np.array([[1, 2], [4, 3]])`
		`>>> np.empty_like(a)`
		`array([[0, 0], [0, 0]])`

eye, identity	Create a NxN identity matrix with ones on the diagonal and zero elsewhere	`>>> np.eye(2, dtype=np.int)` `array([[1, 0], [0, 1]])`

ones, ones_like	Create a new array with the given shape and type, filled with 1s for all elements	`>>> np.ones(5)`
		`array([1., 1., 1., 1., 1.])`
		`>>> np.ones(4, dtype=np.int)`
		`array([1, 1, 1, 1])`
		`>>> x = np.array([[0,1,2], [3,4,5]])`
		`>>> np.ones_like(x)`
		`array([[1, 1, 1],[1, 1, 1]])`

Function	Description	Example

zeros, zeros_like	This is similar to ones, ones_like, but initializing elements with 0s instead	`>>> np.zeros(5)`
		`array([0., 0., 0., 0-, 0.])`
		`>>> np.zeros(4, dtype=np.int)`
		`array([0, 0, 0, 0])`
		`>>> x = np.array([[0, 1, 2], [3, 4, 5]])`
		`>>> np.zeros_like(x)`
		`array([[0, 0, 0],[0, 0, 0]])`

arange	Create an array with even spaced values in a given interval	`>>> np.arange(2, 5)`
		`array([2, 3, 4])`
		`>>> np.arange(4, 12, 5)`
		`array([4, 9])`

full, full_like	Create a new array with the given shape and type, filled with a selected value	`>>> np.full((2,2), 3, dtype=np.int)`
		`array([[3, 3], [3, 3]])`
		`>>> x = np.ones(3)`
		`>>> np.full_like(x, 2)`
		`array([2., 2., 2.])`

array	Create an array from the existing data	`>>> np.array([[1.1, 2.2, 3.3], [4.4, 5.5, 6.6]])` `array([1.1, 2.2, 3.3], [4.4, 5.5, 6.6]])`

asarray	Convert the input to an array	`>>> a = [3.14, 2.46]`
		`>>> np.asarray(a)`
		`array([3.14, 2.46])`

copy	Return an array copy of the given object	`>>> a = np.array([[1, 2], [3, 4]])`
		`>>> np.copy(a)`
		`array([[1, 2], [3, 4]])`

fromstring	Create 1-D array from a string or text	`>>> np.fromstring('3.14 2.17', dtype=np.float, sep=' ')` `array([3.14, 2.17])`

Indexing and slicing

As with other Python sequence types, such as lists, it is very easy to access and assign a value of each array's element:

```
>>> a = np.arange(7)
>>> a
array([0, 1, 2, 3, 4, 5, 6])
>>> a[1], a [4], a[-1]
(1, 4, 6)
```

 In Python, array indices start at 0. This is in contrast to Fortran or Matlab, where indices begin at 1.

As another example, if our array is multidimensional, we need tuples of integers to index an item:

```
>>> a = np.array([[1, 2, 3], [4, 5, 6], [7, 8, 9]])
>>> a[0, 2]        # first row, third column
3
>>> a[0, 2] = 10
>>> a
array([[1, 2, 10], [4, 5, 6], [7, 8, 9]])
>>> b = a[2]
>>> b
array([7, 8, 9])
>>> c = a[:2]
>>> c
array([[1, 2, 10], [4, 5, 6]])
```

We call b and c as array slices, which are views on the original one. It means that the data is not copied to b or c, and whenever we modify their values, it will be reflected in the array a as well:

```
>>> b[-1] = 11
>>> a
array([[1, 2, 10], [4, 5, 6], [7, 8, 11]])
```

 We use a colon (:) character to take the entire axis when we omit the index number.

Fancy indexing

Besides indexing with slices, NumPy also supports indexing with Boolean or integer arrays (masks). This method is called **fancy indexing**. It creates copies, not views.

First, we take a look at an example of indexing with a Boolean mask array:

```
>>> a = np.array([3, 5, 1, 10])
>>> b = (a % 5 == 0)
>>> b
array([False, True, False, True], dtype=bool)
>>> c = np.array([[0, 1], [2, 3], [4, 5], [6, 7]])
>>> c[b]
array([[2, 3], [6, 7]])
```

The second example is an illustration of using integer masks on arrays:

```
>>> a = np.array([[1, 2, 3, 4],
 [5, 6, 7, 8],
 [9, 10, 11, 12],
 [13, 14, 15, 16]])
>>> a[[2, 1]]
array([[9, 10, 11, 12], [5, 6, 7, 8]])
>>> a[[-2, -1]]            # select rows from the end
array([[ 9, 10, 11, 12], [13, 14, 15, 16]])
>>> a[[2, 3], [0, 1]]    # take elements at (2, 0) and (3, 1)
array([9, 14])
```

The mask array must have the same length as the axis that it's indexing.

Downloading the example code

You can download the example code files for all Packt books you have purchased from your account at http://www.packtpub.com. If you purchased this book elsewhere, you can visit http://www.packtpub.com/support and register to have the files e-mailed directly to you.

Numerical operations on arrays

We are getting familiar with creating and accessing ndarrays. Now, we continue to the next step, applying some mathematical operations to array data without writing any for loops, of course, with higher performance.

Scalar operations will propagate the value to each element of the array:

```
>>> a = np.ones(4)
>>> a * 2
array([2., 2., 2., 2.])
>>> a + 3
array([4., 4., 4., 4.])
```

All arithmetic operations between arrays apply the operation element wise:

```
>>> a = np.ones([2, 4])
>>> a * a
array([[1., 1., 1., 1.], [1., 1., 1., 1.]])
>>> a + a
array([[2., 2., 2., 2.], [2., 2., 2., 2.]])
```

Also, here are some examples of comparisons and logical operations:

```
>>> a = np.array([1, 2, 3, 4])
>>> b = np.array([1, 1, 5, 3])
>>> a == b
array([True, False, False, False], dtype=bool)


>>> np.array_equal(a, b)        # array-wise comparison
False


>>> c = np.array([1, 0])
>>> d = np.array([1, 1])
>>> np.logical_and(c, d)        # logical operations
array([True, False])
```

Array functions

Many helpful array functions are supported in NumPy for analyzing data. We will
list some part of them that are common in use. Firstly, the transposing function
is another kind of reshaping form that returns a view on the original data array
without copying anything:

```
>>> a = np.array([[0, 5, 10], [20, 25, 30]])
>>> a.reshape(3, 2)
array([[0, 5], [10, 20], [25, 30]])
>>> a.T
array([[0, 20], [5, 25], [10, 30]])
```

In general, we have the swapaxes method that takes a pair of axis numbers and
returns a view on the data, without making a copy:

```
>>> a = np.array([[[0, 1, 2], [3, 4, 5]],
  [[6, 7, 8], [9, 10, 11]]])
>>> a.swapaxes(1, 2)
array([[[0, 3],
    [1, 4],
    [2, 5]],
   [[6, 9],
    [7, 10],
    [8, 11]]])
```

The transposing function is used to do matrix computations; for example, computing
the inner matrix product XT.X using np.dot:

```
>>> a = np.array([[1, 2, 3],[4,5,6]])
>>> np.dot(a.T, a)
array([[17, 22, 27],
   [22, 29, 36],
   [27, 36, 45]])
```

Sorting data in an array is also an important demand in processing data. Let's take a look at some sorting functions and their use:

```
>>> a = np.array ([[6, 34, 1, 6], [0, 5, 2, -1]])

>>> np.sort(a)      # sort along the last axis
array([[1, 6, 6, 34], [-1, 0, 2, 5]])

>>> np.sort(a, axis=0)     # sort along the first axis
array([[0, 5, 1, -1], [6, 34, 2, 6]])

>>> b = np.argsort(a)     # fancy indexing of sorted array
>>> b
array([[2, 0, 3, 1], [3, 0, 2, 1]])
>>> a[0][b[0]]
array([1, 6, 6, 34])

>>> np.argmax(a)     # get index of maximum element
1
```

See the following table for a listing of array functions:

Function	Description	Example

sin, cos, tan, cosh, sinh, tanh, arcos, arctan, deg2rad	Trigonometric and hyperbolic functions	```>>> a = np.array([0.,30., 45.])```
		```>>> np.sin(a * np.pi / 180)```
		```array([0., 0.5, 0.7071678])```

around, round, rint, fix, floor, ceil, trunc	Rounding elements of an array to the given or nearest number	```>>> a = np.array([0.34, 1.65])```
		```>>> np.round(a)```
		```array([0., 2.])```

sqrt, square, exp, expm1, exp2, log, log10, log1p, logaddexp	Computing the exponents and logarithms of an array	```>>> np.exp(np.array([2.25, 3.16]))``` ```array([9.4877, 23.5705])```

Function	Description	Example

add, negative, multiply, devide, power, substract, mod, modf, remainder	Set of arithmetic functions on arrays	>>> a = np.arange(6)
		>>> x1 = a.reshape(2,3)
		>>> x2 = np.arange(3)
		>>> np.multiply(x1, x2)
		array([[0,1,4],[0,4,10]])

greater, greater_equal, less, less_equal, equal, not_equal	Perform elementwise comparison: >, >=, <, <=, ==, !=	>>> np.greater(x1, x2) array([[False, False, False], [True, True, True]], dtype = bool)

Data processing using arrays

With the NumPy package, we can easily solve many kinds of data processing tasks without writing complex loops. It is very helpful for us to control our code as well as the performance of the program. In this part, we want to introduce some mathematical and statistical functions.

See the following table for a listing of mathematical and statistical functions:

Function	Description	Example

sum	Calculate the sum of all the elements in an array or along the axis	>>> a = np.array([[2,4], [3,5]])
		>>> np.sum(a, axis=0)
		array([5, 9])

prod	Compute the product of array elements over the given axis	>>> np.prod(a, axis=1) array([8, 15])
diff	Calculate the discrete difference along the given axis	>>> np.diff(a, axis=0) array([[1,1]])
gradient	Return the gradient of an array	>>> np.gradient(a) [array([[1., 1.], [1., 1.]]), array([[2., 2.], [2., 2.]])]

cross	Return the cross product of two arrays	>>> b = np.array([[1,2], [3,4]])
		>>> np.cross(a,b)
		array([0, -3])

Function	Description	Example

`std, var`	Return standard deviation and variance of arrays	`>>> np.std(a)`
		
		`1.1180339`
		
		`>>> np.var(a)`
		
		`1.25`

`mean`	Calculate arithmetic mean of an array	`>>> np.mean(a)`
		
		`3.5`

`where`	Return elements, either from x or y, that satisfy a condition	`>>> np.where([[True, True], [False, True]], [[1,2],[3,4]], [[5,6],[7,8]])`
		
		`array([[1,2], [7, 4]])`

`unique`	Return the sorted unique values in an array	`>>> id = np.array(['a', 'b', 'c', 'c', 'd'])`
		
		`>>> np.unique(id)`
		
		`array(['a', 'b', 'c', 'd'], dtype='|S1')`

`intersect1d`	Compute the sorted and common elements in two arrays	`>>> a = np.array(['a', 'b', 'a', 'c', 'd', 'c'])`
		
		`>>> b = np.array(['a', 'xyz', 'klm', 'd'])`
		
		`>>> np.intersect1d(a,b)`
		
		`array(['a', 'd'], dtype='|S3')`

Loading and saving data

We can also save and load data to and from a disk, either in text or binary format, by using different supported functions in NumPy package.

Saving an array

Arrays are saved by default in an uncompressed raw binary format, with the file extension .npy by the np.save function:

```
>>> a = np.array([[0, 1, 2], [3, 4, 5]])
>>> np.save('test1.npy', a)
```

The library automatically assigns the `.npy` extension, if we omit it.

If we want to store several arrays into a single file in an uncompressed `.npz` format, we can use the `np.savez` function, as shown in the following example:

```
>>> a = np.arange(4)
>>> b = np.arange(7)
>>> np.savez('test2.npz', arr0=a, arr1=b)
```

The `.npz` file is a zipped archive of files named after the variables they contain. When we load an `.npz` file, we get back a dictionary-like object that can be queried for its lists of arrays:

```
>>> dic = np.load('test2.npz')
>>> dic['arr0']
array([0, 1, 2, 3])
```

Another way to save array data into a file is using the `np.savetxt` function that allows us to set format properties in the output file:

```
>>> x = np.arange(4)
>>> # e.g., set comma as separator between elements
>>> np.savetxt('test3.out', x, delimiter=',')
```

Loading an array

We have two common functions such as `np.load` and `np.loadtxt`, which correspond to the saving functions, for loading an array:

```
>>> np.load('test1.npy')
array([[0, 1, 2], [3, 4, 5]])
>>> np.loadtxt('test3.out', delimiter=',')
array([0., 1., 2., 3.])
```

Similar to the `np.savetxt` function, the `np.loadtxt` function also has a lot of options for loading an array from a text file.

Linear algebra with NumPy

Linear algebra is a branch of mathematics concerned with vector spaces and the mappings between those spaces. NumPy has a package called **linalg** that supports powerful linear algebra functions. We can use these functions to find eigenvalues and eigenvectors or to perform singular value decomposition:

```
>>> A = np.array([[1, 4, 6],
    [5, 2, 2],
    [-1, 6, 8]])
>>> w, v = np.linalg.eig(A)
>>> w                          # eigenvalues
array([-0.111 + 1.5756j, -0.111 - 1.5756j, 11.222+0.j])
>>> v                          # eigenvector
array([[-0.0981 + 0.2726j, -0.0981 - 0.2726j, 0.5764+0.j],
    [0.7683+0.j, 0.7683-0.j, 0.4591+0.j],
    [-0.5656 - 0.0762j, -0.5656 + 0.00763j, 0.6759+0.j]])
```

The function is implemented using the geev Lapack routines that compute the eigenvalues and eigenvectors of general square matrices.

Another common problem is solving linear systems such as Ax = b with A as a matrix and x and b as vectors. The problem can be solved easily using the numpy.linalg.solve function:

```
>>> A = np.array([[1, 4, 6], [5, 2, 2], [-1, 6, 8]])
>>> b = np.array([[1], [2], [3]])
>>> x = np.linalg.solve(A, b)
>>> x
array([[-1.77635e-16], [2.5], [-1.5]])
```

The following table will summarise some commonly used functions in the numpy.linalg package:

Function	Description	Example

dot	Calculate the dot product of two arrays	`>>> a = np.array([[1, 0],[0, 1]])`
		`>>> b = np.array( [[4, 1],[2, 2]])`
		`>>> np.dot(a,b)`
		`array([[4, 1],[2, 2]])`

Function	Description	Example

inner, outer	Calculate the inner and outer product of two arrays	`>>> a = np.array([1, 1, 1])`
		`>>> b = np.array([3, 5, 1])`
		`>>> np.inner(a,b)`
		`9`

linalg.norm	Find a matrix or vector norm	`>>> a = np.arange(3)`
		`>>> np.linalg.norm(a)`
		`2.23606`

linalg.det	Compute the determinant of an array	`>>> a = np.array([[1,2],[3,4]])`
		`>>> np.linalg.det(a)`
		`-2.0`

linalg.inv	Compute the inverse of a matrix	`>>> a = np.array([[1,2],[3,4]])`
		`>>> np.linalg.inv(a)`
		`array([[-2., 1.],[1.5, -0.5]])`

linalg.qr	Calculate the QR decomposition	`>>> a = np.array([[1,2],[3,4]])`
		`>>> np.linalg.qr(a)`
		`(array([[0.316, 0.948], [0.948, 0.316]]), array([[ 3.162, 4.427], [ 0., 0.632]]))`

linalg.cond	Compute the condition number of a matrix	`>>> a = np.array([[1,3],[2,4]])`
		`>>> np.linalg.cond(a)`
		`14.933034`

trace	Compute the sum of the diagonal element	`>>> np.trace(np.arange(6).reshape(2,3))` `4`

NumPy random numbers

An important part of any simulation is the ability to generate random numbers. For this purpose, NumPy provides various routines in the submodule `random`. It uses a particular algorithm, called the Mersenne Twister, to generate pseudorandom numbers.

First, we need to define a seed that makes the random numbers predictable. When the value is reset, the same numbers will appear every time. If we do not assign the seed, NumPy automatically selects a random seed value based on the system's random number generator device or on the clock:

```
>>> np.random.seed(20)
```

An array of random numbers in the [0.0, 1.0] interval can be generated as follows:

```
>>> np.random.rand(5)
array([0.5881308, 0.89771373, 0.89153073, 0.81583748,
        0.03588959])
>>> np.random.rand(5)
array([0.69175758, 0.37868094, 0.51851095, 0.65795147,
        0.19385022])

>>> np.random.seed(20)     # reset seed number
>>> np.random.rand(5)
array([0.5881308, 0.89771373, 0.89153073, 0.81583748,
        0.03588959])
```

If we want to generate random integers in the half-open interval [min, max], we can user the randint(min, max, length) function:

```
>>> np.random.randint(10, 20, 5)
array([17, 12, 10, 16, 18])
```

NumPy also provides for many other distributions, including the Beta, bionomial, chi-square, Dirichlet, exponential, F, Gamma, geometric, or Gumbel.

The following table will list some distribution functions and give examples for generating random numbers:

Function	Description	Example

binomial	Draw samples from a binomial distribution (n: number of trials, p: probability)	`>>> n, p = 100, 0.2`
		`>>> np.random.binomial(n, p, 3)`
		`array([17, 14, 23])`

dirichlet	Draw samples using a Dirichlet distribution	`>>> np.random.`
		`dirichlet(alpha=(2,3), size=3)`
		`array([[0.519, 0.480], [0.639,`
		`0.36],`
		`[0.838, 0.161]])`

poisson	Draw samples from a Poisson distribution	`>>> np.random.poisson(lam=2, size=`
		`2)`
		`array([4,1])`

normal	Draw samples using a normal Gaussian distribution	`>>> np.random.normal`
		`(loc=2.5, scale=0.3, size=3)`
		`array([2.4436, 2.849, 2.741)`

uniform	Draw samples using a uniform distribution	`>>> np.random.uniform(`
		`low=0.5, high=2.5, size=3)`
		`array([1.38, 1.04, 2.19[)`

We can also use the random number generation to shuffle items in a list. Sometimes this is useful when we want to sort a list in a random order:

```
>>> a = np.arange(10)
>>> np.random.shuffle(a)
>>> a
array([7, 6, 3, 1, 4, 2, 5, 0, 9, 8])
```

The following figure shows two distributions, `binomial` and `poisson`, side by side with various parameters (the visualization was created with `matplotlib`, which will be covered in *Chapter 4, Data Visualization*):

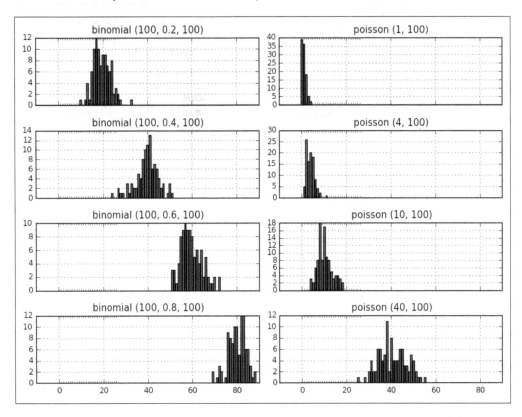

Summary

In this chapter, we covered a lot of information related to the NumPy package, especially commonly used functions that are very helpful to process and analyze data in `ndarray`. Firstly, we learned the properties and data type of `ndarray` in the NumPy package. Secondly, we focused on how to create and manipulate an `ndarray` in different ways, such as conversion from other structures, reading an array from disk, or just generating a new array with given values. Thirdly, we studied how to access and control the value of each element in `ndarray` by using indexing and slicing.

Then, we are getting familiar with some common functions and operations on ndarray.

And finally, we continue with some advance functions that are related to statistic, linear algebra and sampling data. Those functions play important role in data analysis.

However, while NumPy by itself does not provide very much high-level data analytical functionality, having an understanding of it will help you use tools such as Pandas much more effectively. This tool will be discussed in the next chapter.

Practice exercises

Exercise 1: Using an array creation function, let's try to create arrays variable in the following situations:

- Create ndarray from the existing data
- Initialize ndarray which elements are filled with ones, zeros, or a given interval
- Loading and saving data from a file to an ndarray

Exercise 2: What is the difference between np.dot(a, b) and (a*b)?

Exercise 3: Consider the vector [1, 2, 3, 4, 5] building a new vector with four consecutive zeros interleaved between each value.

Exercise 4: Taking the data example file chapter2-data.txt, which includes information on a system log, solves the following tasks:

- Try to build an ndarray from the data file
- Statistic frequency of each device type in the built matrix
- List unique OS that appears in the data log
- Sort user by provinceID and count the number of users in each province

3
Data Analysis with Pandas

In this chapter, we will explore another data analysis library called Pandas. The goal of this chapter is to give you some basic knowledge and concrete examples for getting started with Pandas.

An overview of the Pandas package

Pandas is a Python package that supports fast, flexible, and expressive data structures, as well as computing functions for data analysis. The following are some prominent features that Pandas supports:

- Data structure with labeled axes. This makes the program clean and clear and avoids common errors from misaligned data.
- Flexible handling of missing data.
- Intelligent label-based slicing, fancy indexing, and subset creation of large datasets.
- Powerful arithmetic operations and statistical computations on a custom axis via axis label.
- Robust input and output support for loading or saving data from and to files, databases, or HDF5 format.

Related to Pandas installation, we recommend an easy way, that is to install it as a part of Anaconda, a cross-platform distribution for data analysis and scientific computing. You can refer to the reference at http://docs.continuum.io/anaconda/ to download and install the library.

After installation, we can use it like other Python packages. Firstly, we have to import the following packages at the beginning of the program:

```
>>> import pandas as pd
>>> import numpy as np
```

The Pandas data structure

Let's first get acquainted with two of Pandas' primary data structures: the Series and the DataFrame. They can handle the majority of use cases in finance, statistic, social science, and many areas of engineering.

Series

A Series is a one-dimensional object similar to an array, list, or column in table. Each item in a Series is assigned to an entry in an index:

```
>>> s1 = pd.Series(np.random.rand(4),
                   index=['a', 'b', 'c', 'd'])
>>> s1
a    0.6122
b    0.98096
c    0.3350
d    0.7221
dtype: float64
```

By default, if no index is passed, it will be created to have values ranging from 0 to N-1, where N is the length of the Series:

```
>>> s2 = pd.Series(np.random.rand(4))
>>> s2
0    0.6913
1    0.8487
2    0.8627
3    0.7286
dtype: float64
```

We can access the value of a Series by using the index:

```
>>> s1['c']
0.3350
>>>s1['c'] = 3.14
>>> s1['c', 'a', 'b']
c     3.14
a     0.6122
b     0.98096
```

This accessing method is similar to a Python dictionary. Therefore, Pandas also allows us to initialize a Series object directly from a Python dictionary:

```
>>> s3 = pd.Series({'001': 'Nam', '002': 'Mary',
                    '003': 'Peter'})
>>> s3
001     Nam
002     Mary
003     Peter
dtype: object
```

Sometimes, we want to filter or rename the index of a Series created from a Python dictionary. At such times, we can pass the selected index list directly to the initial function, similarly to the process in the above example. Only elements that exist in the index list will be in the Series object. Conversely, indexes that are missing in the dictionary are initialized to default NaN values by Pandas:

```
>>> s4 = pd.Series({'001': 'Nam', '002': 'Mary',
                    '003': 'Peter'}, index=[
                    '002', '001', '024', '065'])
>>> s4
002     Mary
001     Nam
024     NaN
065     NaN
dtype:    object
ect
```

The library also supports functions that detect missing data:

```
>>> pd.isnull(s4)
002      False
001      False
024      True
065      True
dtype: bool
```

Similarly, we can also initialize a Series from a scalar value:

```
>>> s5 = pd.Series(2.71, index=['x', 'y'])
>>> s5
x      2.71
y      2.71
dtype: float64
```

A Series object can be initialized with NumPy objects as well, such as `ndarray`. Moreover, Pandas can automatically align data indexed in different ways in arithmetic operations:

```
>>> s6 = pd.Series(np.array([2.71, 3.14]), index=['z', 'y'])
>>> s6
z      2.71
y      3.14
dtype: float64
>>> s5 + s6
x      NaN
y      5.85
z      NaN
dtype: float64
```

The DataFrame

The DataFrame is a tabular data structure comprising a set of ordered columns and rows. It can be thought of as a group of Series objects that share an index (the column names). There are a number of ways to initialize a DataFrame object. Firstly, let's take a look at the common example of creating DataFrame from a dictionary of lists:

```
>>> data = {'Year': [2000, 2005, 2010, 2014],
            'Median_Age': [24.2, 26.4, 28.5, 30.3],
```

```
            'Density': [244, 256, 268, 279]}
>>> df1 = pd.DataFrame(data)
>>> df1
    Density      Median_Age      Year
0   244          24.2            2000
1   256          26.4            2005
2   268          28.5            2010
3   279          30.3            2014
```

By default, the DataFrame constructor will order the column alphabetically. We can edit the default order by passing the column's attribute to the initializing function:

```
>>> df2 = pd.DataFrame(data, columns=['Year', 'Density',
                                      'Median_Age'])
>>> df2
    Year      Density      Median_Age
0   2000      244          24.2
1   2005      256          26.4
2   2010      268          28.5
3   2014      279          30.3
>>> df2.index
Int64Index([0, 1, 2, 3], dtype='int64')
```

We can provide the index labels of a DataFrame similar to a Series:

```
>>> df3 = pd.DataFrame(data, columns=['Year', 'Density',
                'Median_Age'], index=['a', 'b', 'c', 'd'])
>>> df3.index
Index([u'a', u'b', u'c', u'd'], dtype='object')
```

We can construct a DataFrame out of nested lists as well:

```
>>> df4 = pd.DataFrame([
    ['Peter', 16, 'pupil', 'TN', 'M', None],
    ['Mary', 21, 'student', 'SG', 'F', None],
    ['Nam', 22, 'student', 'HN', 'M', None],
    ['Mai', 31, 'nurse', 'SG', 'F', None],
    ['John', 28, 'laywer', 'SG', 'M', None]],
columns=['name', 'age', 'career', 'province', 'sex', 'award'])
```

Columns can be accessed by column name as a Series can, either by dictionary-like notation or as an attribute, if the column name is a syntactically valid attribute name:

```
>>> df4.name    # or df4['name']
0     Peter
1     Mary
2     Nam
3     Mai
4     John
Name: name, dtype: object
```

To modify or append a new column to the created DataFrame, we specify the column name and the value we want to assign:

```
>>> df4['award'] = None
>>> df4
    name age   career province  sex award
0  Peter  16    pupil       TN    M  None
1   Mary  21  student       SG    F  None
2    Nam  22  student       HN    M  None
3    Mai  31    nurse       SG    F  None
4   John  28    lawer       SG    M  None
```

Using a couple of methods, rows can be retrieved by position or name:

```
>>> df4.ix[1]
name           Mary
age              21
career      student
province         SG
sex               F
award          None
Name: 1, dtype: object
```

A DataFrame object can also be created from different data structures such as a list of dictionaries, a dictionary of Series, or a record array. The method to initialize a DataFrame object is similar to the examples above.

Another common case is to provide a DataFrame with data from a location such as a text file. In this situation, we use the `read_csv` function that expects the column separator to be a comma, by default. However, we can change that by using the `sep` parameter:

```
# person.csv file
name,age,career,province,sex
Peter,16,pupil,TN,M
Mary,21,student,SG,F
Nam,22,student,HN,M
Mai,31,nurse,SG,F
John,28,lawer,SG,M
# loading person.cvs into a DataFrame
>>> df4 = pd.read_csv('person.csv')
>>> df4
```

	name	age	career	province	sex
0	Peter	16	pupil	TN	M
1	Mary	21	student	SG	F
2	Nam	22	student	HN	M
3	Mai	31	nurse	SG	F
4	John	28	laywer	SG	M

While reading a data file, we sometimes want to skip a line or an invalid value. As for Pandas `0.16.2`, `read_csv` supports over 50 parameters for controlling the loading process. Some common useful parameters are as follows:

- `sep`: This is a delimiter between columns. The default is comma symbol.
- `dtype`: This is a data type for data or columns.
- `header`: This sets row numbers to use as the column names.
- `skiprows`: This skips line numbers to skip at the start of the file.
- `error_bad_lines`: This shows invalid lines (too many fields) that will, by default, cause an exception, such that no DataFrame will be returned. If we set the value of this parameter as `false`, the bad lines will be skipped.

Moreover, Pandas also has support for reading and writing a DataFrame directly from or to a database such as the `read_frame` or `write_frame` function within the Pandas module. We will come back to these methods later in this chapter.

The essential basic functionality

Pandas supports many essential functionalities that are useful to manipulate Pandas data structures. In this book, we will focus on the most important features regarding exploration and analysis.

Reindexing and altering labels

Reindex is a critical method in the Pandas data structures. It confirms whether the new or modified data satisfies a given set of labels along a particular axis of Pandas object.

First, let's view a `reindex` example on a Series object:

```
>>> s2.reindex([0, 2, 'b', 3])
0      0.6913
2      0.8627
b      NaN
3      0.7286
dtype: float64
```

When `reindexed` labels do not exist in the data object, a default value of NaN will be automatically assigned to the position; this holds true for the DataFrame case as well:

```
>>> df1.reindex(index=[0, 2, 'b', 3],
         columns=['Density', 'Year', 'Median_Age','C'])
    Density  Year  Median_Age      C
0       244  2000        24.2    NaN
2       268  2010        28.5    NaN
b       NaN   NaN         NaN    NaN
3       279  2014        30.3    NaN
```

We can change the NaN value in the missing index case to a custom value by setting the `fill_value` parameter. Let us take a look at the arguments that the `reindex` function supports, as shown in the following table:

Argument	Description
index	This is the new labels/index to conform to.
method	This is the method to use for filling holes in a `reindexed` object. The default setting is unfill gaps. `pad`/`ffill`: fill values forward `backfill`/`bfill`: fill values backward `nearest`: use the nearest value to fill the gap
copy	This return a new object. The default setting is `true`.
level	The matches index values on the passed multiple index level.
fill_value	This is the value to use for missing values. The default setting is NaN.
limit	This is the maximum size gap to fill in `forward` or `backward` method.

Head and tail

In common data analysis situations, our data structure objects contain many columns and a large number of rows. Therefore, we cannot view or load all information of the objects. Pandas supports functions that allow us to inspect a small sample. By default, the functions return five elements, but we can set a custom number as well. The following example shows how to display the first five and the last three rows of a longer Series:

```
>>> s7 = pd.Series(np.random.rand(10000))
>>> s7.head()
0    0.631059
1    0.766085
2    0.066891
3    0.867591
4    0.339678
```

```
dtype: float64
>>> s7.tail(3)
9997      0.412178
9998      0.800711
9999      0.438344
dtype: float64
```

We can also use these functions for DataFrame objects in the same way.

Binary operations

Firstly, we will consider arithmetic operations between objects. In different indexes objects case, the expected result will be the union of the index pairs. We will not explain this again because we had an example about it in the above section (s5 + s6). This time, we will show another example with a DataFrame:

```
>>> df5 = pd.DataFrame(np.arange(9).reshape(3,3),0
                       columns=['a','b','c'])
>>> df5
   a  b  c
0  0  1  2
1  3  4  5
2  6  7  8
>>> df6 = pd.DataFrame(np.arange(8).reshape(2,4),
                       columns=['a','b','c','d'])
>>> df6
   a  b  c  d
0  0  1  2  3
1  4  5  6  7
>>> df5 + df6
   a    b    c    d
0  0    2    4  NaN
1  7    9   11  NaN
2  NaN NaN NaN NaN
```

The mechanisms for returning the result between two kinds of data structure are similar. A problem that we need to consider is the missing data between objects. In this case, if we want to fill with a fixed value, such as 0, we can use the arithmetic functions such as add, sub, div, and mul, and the function's supported parameters such as fill_value:

```
>>> df7 = df5.add(df6, fill_value=0)
>>> df7
   a  b   c    d
0  0  2   4    3
1  7  9  11    7
2  6  7   8  NaN
```

Next, we will discuss comparison operations between data objects. We have some supported functions such as **equal (eq)**, **not equal (ne)**, **greater than (gt)**, **less than (lt)**, **less equal (le)**, and **greater equal (ge)**. Here is an example:

```
>>> df5.eq(df6)
       a      b      c      d
0   True   True   True  False
1  False  False  False  False
2  False  False  False  False
```

Functional statistics

The supported statistics method of a library is really important in data analysis. To get inside a big data object, we need to know some summarized information such as mean, sum, or quantile. Pandas supports a large number of methods to compute them. Let's consider a simple example of calculating the sum information of df5, which is a DataFrame object:

```
>>> df5.sum()
a     9
b    12
c    15
dtype: int64
```

When we do not specify which axis we want to calculate `sum` information, by default, the function will calculate on index axis, which is axis `0`:

- **Series**: We do not need to specify the axis.
- **DataFrame**: Columns (`axis = 1`) or index (`axis = 0`). The default setting is `axis 0`.

We also have the `skipna` parameter that allows us to decide whether to exclude missing data or not. By default, it is set as `true`:

```
>>> df7.sum(skipna=False)
a      13
b      18
c      23
d      NaN
dtype: float64
```

Another function that we want to consider is `describe()`. It is very convenient for us to summarize most of the statistical information of a data structure such as the Series and DataFrame, as well:

```
>>> df5.describe()
          a      b      c
count   3.0    3.0    3.0
mean    3.0    4.0    5.0
std     3.0    3.0    3.0
min     0.0    1.0    2.0
25%     1.5    2.5    3.5
50%     3.0    4.0    5.0
75%     4.5    5.5    6.5
max     6.0    7.0    8.0
```

We can specify percentiles to include or exclude in the output by using the `percentiles` parameter; for example, consider the following:

```
>>> df5.describe(percentiles=[0.5, 0.8])
          a      b      c
count   3.0    3.0    3.0
mean    3.0    4.0    5.0
std     3.0    3.0    3.0
```

```
min      0.0   1.0   2.0
50%      3.0   4.0   5.0
80%      4.8   5.8   6.8
max      6.0   7.0   8.0
```

Here, we have a summary table for common supported statistics functions in Pandas:

Function	Description
`idxmin(axis)`, `idxmax(axis)`	This compute the index labels with the minimum or maximum corresponding values.
`value_counts()`	This compute the frequency of unique values.
`count()`	This return the number of non-null values in a data object.
`mean()`, `median()`, `min()`, `max()`	This return mean, median, minimum, and maximum values of an axis in a data object.
`std()`, `var()`, `sem()`	These return the standard deviation, variance, and standard error of mean.
`abs()`	This gets the absolute value of a data object.

Function application

Pandas supports function application that allows us to apply some functions supported in other packages such as NumPy or our own functions on data structure objects. Here, we illustrate two examples of these cases, firstly, using `apply` to execute the `std()` function, which is the standard deviation calculating function of the NumPy package:

```
>>> df5.apply(np.std, axis=1)      # default: axis=0
0      0.816497
1      0.816497
2      0.816497
dtype: float64
```

Secondly, if we want to apply a formula to a data object, we can also use apply function by following these steps:

1. Define the function or formula that you want to apply on a data object.

2. Call the defined function or formula via `apply`. In this step, we also need to figure out the axis that we want to apply the calculation to:

```
>>> f = lambda x: x.max() - x.min()      # step 1
>>> df5.apply(f, axis=1)                  # step 2
0    2
1    2
2    2
dtype: int64
>>> def sigmoid(x):
        return 1/(1 + np.exp(x))
>>> df5.apply(sigmoid)
          a         b         c
0  0.500000  0.268941  0.119203
1  0.047426  0.017986  0.006693
2  0.002473  0.000911  0.000335
```

Sorting

There are two kinds of sorting method that we are interested in: sorting by row or column index and sorting by data value.

Firstly, we will consider methods for sorting by row and column index. In this case, we have the `sort_index ()` function. We also have `axis` parameter to set whether the function should sort by row or column. The `ascending` option with the `true` or `false` value will allow us to sort data in ascending or descending order. The default setting for this option is `true`:

```
>>> df7 = pd.DataFrame(np.arange(12).reshape(3,4),
                       columns=['b', 'd', 'a', 'c'],
                       index=['x', 'y', 'z'])
>>> df7
   b  d   a   c
x  0  1   2   3
y  4  5   6   7
z  8  9  10  11
```

```
>>> df7.sort_index(axis=1)
     a   b   c   d
x    2   0   3   1
y    6   4   7   5
z   10   8  11   9
```

Series has a method order that sorts by value. For NaN values in the object, we can also have a special treatment via the na_position option:

```
>>> s4.order(na_position='first')
024      NaN
065      NaN
002      Mary
001      Nam
dtype: object
>>> s4
002      Mary
001      Nam
024      NaN
065      NaN
dtype: object
```

Besides that, Series also has the sort() function that sorts data by value. However, the function will not return a copy of the sorted data:

```
>>> s4.sort(na_position='first')
>>> s4
024      NaN
065      NaN
002      Mary
001      Nam
dtype: object
```

If we want to apply sort function to a DataFrame object, we need to figure out which columns or rows will be sorted:

```
>>> df7.sort(['b', 'd'], ascending=False)
   b  d  a   c
z  8  9  10  11
y  4  5  6   7
x  0  1  2   3
```

If we do not want to automatically save the sorting result to the current data object, we can change the setting of the inplace parameter to False.

Indexing and selecting data

In this section, we will focus on how to get, set, or slice subsets of Pandas data structure objects. As we learned in previous sections, Series or DataFrame objects have axis labeling information. This information can be used to identify items that we want to select or assign a new value to in the object:

```
>>> s4[['024', '002']]     # selecting data of Series object
024      NaN
002      Mary
dtype: object
>>> s4[['024', '002']] = 'unknown' # assigning data
>>> s4
024      unknown
065          NaN
002      unknown
001          Nam
dtype: object
```

If the data object is a DataFrame structure, we can also proceed in a similar way:

```
>>> df5[['b', 'c']]
   b  c
0  1  2
1  4  5
2  7  8
```

For label indexing on the rows of DataFrame, we use the `ix` function that enables us to select a set of rows and columns in the object. There are two parameters that we need to specify: the `row` and `column` labels that we want to get. By default, if we do not specify the selected column names, the function will return selected rows with all columns in the object:

```
>>> df5.ix[0]
a    0
b    1
c    2
Name: 0, dtype: int64
>>> df5.ix[0, 1:3]
b    1
c    2
Name: 0, dtype: int64
```

Moreover, we have many ways to select and edit data contained in a Pandas object. We summarize these functions in the following table:

Method	Description
`icol, irow`	This selects a single row or column by integer location.
`get_value, set_value`	This selects or sets a single value of a data object by row or column label.
`xs`	This selects a single column or row as a Series by label.

Pandas data objects may contain duplicate indices. In this case, when we get or set a data value via index label, it will affect all rows or columns that have the same selected index name.

Computational tools

Let's start with correlation and covariance computation between two data objects. Both the Series and DataFrame have a `cov` method. On a DataFrame object, this method will compute the covariance between the Series inside the object:

```
>>> s1 = pd.Series(np.random.rand(3))
>>> s1
```

```
0    0.460324
1    0.993279
2    0.032957
dtype: float64
>>> s2 = pd.Series(np.random.rand(3))
>>> s2
0    0.777509
1    0.573716
2    0.664212
dtype: float64
>>> s1.cov(s2)
-0.024516360159045424


>>> df8 = pd.DataFrame(np.random.rand(12).reshape(4,3),
                        columns=['a','b','c'])
>>> df8
          a          b          c
0   0.200049   0.070034   0.978615
1   0.293063   0.609812   0.788773
2   0.853431   0.243656   0.978057
0.985584   0.500765   0.481180
>>> df8.cov()
           a          b          c
a   0.155307   0.021273  -0.048449
b   0.021273   0.059925  -0.040029
c  -0.048449  -0.040029   0.055067
```

Usage of the correlation method is similar to the covariance method. It computes the correlation between Series inside a data object in case the data object is a DataFrame. However, we need to specify which method will be used to compute the correlations. The available methods are `pearson`, `kendall`, and `spearman`. By default, the function applies the `spearman` method:

```
>>> df8.corr(method = 'spearman')
     a    b    c
a   1.0  0.4 -0.8
b   0.4  1.0 -0.8
c  -0.8 -0.8  1.0
```

We also have the `corrwith` function that supports calculating correlations between Series that have the same label contained in different DataFrame objects:

```
>>> df9 = pd.DataFrame(np.arange(8).reshape(4,2),
                       columns=['a', 'b'])
>>> df9
   a  b
0  0  1
1  2  3
2  4  5
3  6  7
>>> df8.corrwith(df9)
a      0.955567
b      0.488370
c           NaN
dtype: float64
```

Working with missing data

In this section, we will discuss missing, NaN, or null values, in Pandas data structures. It is a very common situation to arrive with missing data in an object. One such case that creates missing data is reindexing:

```
>>> df8 = pd.DataFrame(np.arange(12).reshape(4,3),
                       columns=['a', 'b', 'c'])
   a   b   c
0  0   1   2
1  3   4   5
2  6   7   8
3  9  10  11
>>> df9 = df8.reindex(columns = ['a', 'b', 'c', 'd'])
   a   b   c   d
0  0   1   2 NaN
1  3   4   5 NaN
2  6   7   8 NaN
4  9  10  11 NaN
```

```
>>> df10 = df8.reindex([3, 2, 'a', 0])
     a    b    c
3    9   10   11
2    6    7    8
a  NaN  NaN  NaN
0    0    1    2
```

To manipulate missing values, we can use the isnull() or notnull() functions to detect the missing values in a Series object, as well as in a DataFrame object:

```
>>> df10.isnull()
        a       b       c
3   False   False   False
2   False   False   False
a    True    True    True
0   False   False   False
```

On a Series, we can drop all null data and index values by using the dropna function:

```
>>> s4 = pd.Series({'001': 'Nam', '002': 'Mary',
                    '003': 'Peter'},
                    index=['002', '001', '024', '065'])
>>> s4
002     Mary
001      Nam
024      NaN
065      NaN
dtype: object
>>> s4.dropna()     # dropping all null value of Series object
002     Mary
001      Nam
dtype: object
```

With a DataFrame object, it is a little bit more complex than with Series. We can tell which rows or columns we want to drop and also if all entries must be `null` or a single `null` value is enough. By default, the function will drop any row containing a missing value:

```
>>> df9.dropna()      # all rows will be dropped
Empty DataFrame
Columns: [a, b, c, d]
Index: []
>>> df9.dropna(axis=1)
   a   b   c
0  0   1   2
1  3   4   5
2  6   7   8
3  9  10  11
```

Another way to control missing values is to use the supported parameters of functions that we introduced in the previous section. They are also very useful to solve this problem. In our experience, we should assign a fixed value in missing cases when we create data objects. This will make our objects cleaner in later processing steps. For example, consider the following:

```
>>> df11 = df8.reindex([3, 2, 'a', 0], fill_value = 0)
>>> df11
   a   b   c
3  9  10  11
2  6   7   8
a  0   0   0
0  0   1   2
```

We can alse use the `fillna` function to fill a custom value in missing values:

```
>>> df9.fillna(-1)
   a   b   c   d
0  0   1   2  -1
1  3   4   5  -1
2  6   7   8  -1
3  9  10  11  -1
```

Advanced uses of Pandas for data analysis

In this section we will consider some advanced Pandas use cases.

Hierarchical indexing

Hierarchical indexing provides us with a way to work with higher dimensional data in a lower dimension by structuring the data object into multiple index levels on an axis:

```
>>> s8 = pd.Series(np.random.rand(8), index=[['a','a','b','b','c','c',
'd','d'], [0, 1, 0, 1, 0,1, 0, 1, ]])
>>> s8
a  0     0.721652
   1     0.297784
b  0     0.271995
   1     0.125342
c  0     0.444074
   1     0.948363
d  0     0.197565
   1     0.883776
dtype: float64
```

In the preceding example, we have a Series object that has two index levels. The object can be rearranged into a DataFrame using the `unstack` function. In an inverse situation, the `stack` function can be used:

```
>>> s8.unstack()
          0          1
a  0.549211   0.420874
b  0.051516   0.715021
c  0.503072   0.720772
d  0.373037   0.207026
```

We can also create a DataFrame to have a hierarchical index in both axes:

```
>>> df = pd.DataFrame(np.random.rand(12).reshape(4,3),
                      index=[['a', 'a', 'b', 'b'],
                             [0, 1, 0, 1]],
                      columns=[['x', 'x', 'y'], [0, 1, 0]])
>>> df
              x                   y
              0         1         0
a 0   0.636893  0.729521  0.747230
  1   0.749002  0.323388  0.259496
b 0   0.214046  0.926961  0.679686
0.013258   0.416101   0.626927
>>> df.index
MultiIndex(levels=[['a', 'b'], [0, 1]],
          labels=[[0, 0, 1, 1], [0, 1, 0, 1]])
>>> df.columns
MultiIndex(levels=[['x', 'y'], [0, 1]],
          labels=[[0, 0, 1], [0, 1, 0]])
```

The methods for getting or setting values or subsets of the data objects with multiple index levels are similar to those of the nonhierarchical case:

```
>>> df['x']
              0         1
a 0   0.636893  0.729521
  1   0.749002  0.323388
b 0   0.214046  0.926961
0.013258   0.416101
>>> df[[0]]
              x
              0
a 0   0.636893
  1   0.749002
b 0   0.214046
0.013258
```

```
>>> df.ix['a', 'x']
          0          1
0   0.636893   0.729521
0.749002   0.323388
>>> df.ix['a','x'].ix[1]
0      0.749002
1      0.323388
Name: 1, dtype: float64
```

After grouping data into multiple index levels, we can also use most of the descriptive and statistics functions that have a level option, which can be used to specify the level we want to process:

```
>>> df.std(level=1)
            x                      y
            0          1           0
0   0.298998   0.139611   0.047761
0.520250   0.065558   0.259813
>>> df.std(level=0)
            x                      y
            0          1           0
a   0.079273   0.287180   0.344880
b   0.141979   0.361232   0.037306
```

The Panel data

The Panel is another data structure for three-dimensional data in Pandas. However, it is less frequently used than the Series or the DataFrame. You can think of a Panel as a table of DataFrame objects. We can create a Panel object from a 3D `ndarray` or a dictionary of DataFrame objects:

```
# create a Panel from 3D ndarray
>>> panel = pd.Panel(np.random.rand(2, 4, 5),
                     items = ['item1', 'item2'])
>>> panel
<class 'pandas.core.panel.Panel'>
Dimensions: 2 (items) x 4 (major_axis) x 5 (minor_axis)
Items axis: item1 to item2
Major_axis axis: 0 to 3
```

```
Minor_axis axis: 0 to 4


>>> df1 = pd.DataFrame(np.arange(12).reshape(4, 3),
                       columns=['a','b','c'])
>>> df1
   a   b   c
0  0   1   2
1  3   4   5
2  6   7   8
9  10  11
>>> df2 = pd.DataFrame(np.arange(9).reshape(3, 3),
                       columns=['a','b','c'])
>>> df2
   a  b  c
0  0  1  2
1  3  4  5
6  7  8
# create another Panel from a dict of DataFrame objects
>>> panel2 = pd.Panel({'item1': df1, 'item2': df2})
>>> panel2
<class 'pandas.core.panel.Panel'>
Dimensions: 2 (items) x 4 (major_axis) x 3 (minor_axis)
Items axis: item1 to item2
Major_axis axis: 0 to 3
Minor_axis axis: a to c
```

Each item in a Panel is a DataFrame. We can select an item, by item name:

```
>>> panel2['item1']
   a   b   c
0  0   1   2
1  3   4   5
2  6   7   8
3  9   10  11
```

Alternatively, if we want to select data via an axis or data position, we can use the `ix` method, like on Series or DataFrame:

```
>>> panel2.ix[:, 1:3, ['b', 'c']]
<class 'pandas.core.panel.Panel'>
Dimensions: 2 (items) x 3 (major_axis) x 2 (minor_axis)
Items axis: item1 to item2
Major_axis axis: 1 to 3
Minor_axis axis: b to c
>>> panel2.ix[:, 2, :]
    item1   item2
a      6       6
b      7       7
c      8       8
```

Summary

We have finished covering the basics of the Pandas data analysis library. Whenever you learn about a library for data analysis, you need to consider the three parts that we explained in this chapter. Data structures: we have two common data object types in the Pandas library; Series and DataFrames. Method to access and manipulate data objects: Pandas supports many way to select, set or slice subsets of data object. However, the general mechanism is using index labels or the positions of items to identify values. Functions and utilities: They are the most important part of a powerful library. In this chapter, we covered all common supported functions of Pandas which allow us compute statistics on data easily. The library also has a lot of other useful functions and utilities that we could not explain in this chapter. We encourage you to start your own research, if you want to expand your experience with Pandas. It helps us to process large data in an optimized way. You will see more of Pandas in action later in this book.

Until now, we learned about two popular Python libraries: NumPy and Pandas. Pandas is built on NumPy, and as a result it allows for a bit more convenient interaction with data. However, in some situations, we can flexibly combine both of them to accomplish our goals.

Practice exercises

The link `https://www.census.gov/2010census/csv/pop_change.csv` contains an US census dataset. It has 23 columns and one row for each US state, as well as a few rows for macro regions such as North, South, and West.

- Get this dataset into a Pandas DataFrame. Hint: just skip those rows that do not seem helpful, such as comments or description.

- While the dataset contains change metrics for each decade, we are interested in the population change during the second half of the twentieth century, that is between, 1950 and 2000. Which region has seen the biggest and the smallest population growth in this time span? Also, which US state?

Advanced open-ended exercise:

- Find more census data on the internet; not just on the US but on the world's countries. Try to find GDP data for the same time as well. Try to align this data to explore patterns. How are GDP and population growth related? Are there any special cases. such as countries with high GDP but low population growth or countries with the opposite history?

4
Data Visualization

Data visualization is concerned with the presentation of data in a pictorial or graphical form. It is one of the most important tasks in data analysis, since it enables us to see analytical results, detect outliers, and make decisions for model building. There are many Python libraries for visualization, of which matplotlib, seaborn, bokeh, and ggplot are among the most popular. However, in this chapter, we mainly focus on the matplotlib library that is used by many people in many different contexts.

Matplotlib produces publication-quality figures in a variety of formats, and interactive environments across Python platforms. Another advantage is that Pandas comes equipped with useful wrappers around several matplotlib plotting routines, allowing for quick and handy plotting of Series and DataFrame objects.

The IPython package started as an alternative to the standard interactive Python shell, but has since evolved into an indispensable tool for data exploration, visualization, and rapid prototyping. It is possible to use the graphical capabilities offered by matplotlib from IPython through various options, of which the simplest to get started with is the `pylab` flag:

```
$ ipython --pylab
```

This flag will preload `matplotlib` and `numpy` for interactive use with the default matplotlib backend. IPython can run in various environments: in a terminal, as a `Qt` application, or inside a browser. These options are worth exploring, since IPython has enjoyed adoption for many use cases, such as prototyping, interactive slides for more engaging conference talks or lectures, and as a tool for sharing research.

The matplotlib API primer

The easiest way to get started with plotting using matplotlib is often by using the MATLAB API that is supported by the package:

```
>>> import matplotlib.pyplot as plt
>>> from numpy import *
>>> x = linspace(0, 3, 6)
>>> x
array([0., 0.6, 1.2, 1.8, 2.4, 3.])
>>> y = power(x,2)
>>> y
array([0., 0.36, 1.44, 3.24, 5.76, 9.])
>>> figure()
>>> plot(x, y, 'r')
>>> xlabel('x')
>>> ylabel('y')
>>> title('Data visualization in MATLAB-like API')
>>> plt.show()
```

The output for the preceding command is as follows:

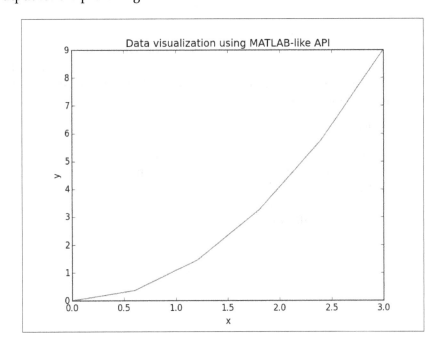

However, star imports should not be used unless there is a good reason for doing so. In the case of matplotlib, we can use the canonical import:

```
>>> import matplotlib.pyplot as plt
```

The preceding example could then be written as follows:

```
>>> plt.plot(x, y)
>>> plt.xlabel('x')
>>> plt.ylabel('y')
>>> plt.title('Data visualization using Pyplot of Matplotlib')
>>> plt.show()
```

The output for the preceding command is as follows:

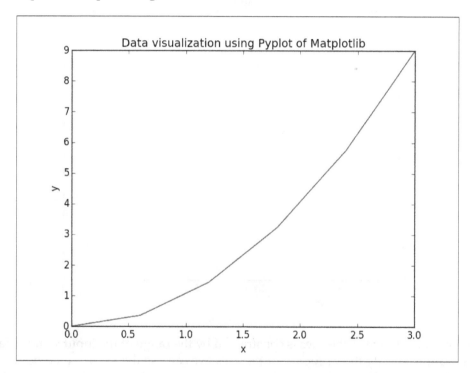

If we only provide a single argument to the plot function, it will automatically use it as the y values and generate the x values from 0 to N-1, where N is equal to the number of values:

```
>>> plt.plot(y)
>>> plt.xlabel('x')
>>> plt.ylabel('y')
>>> plt.title('Plot y value without given x values')
>>> plt.show()
```

The output for the preceding command is as follows:

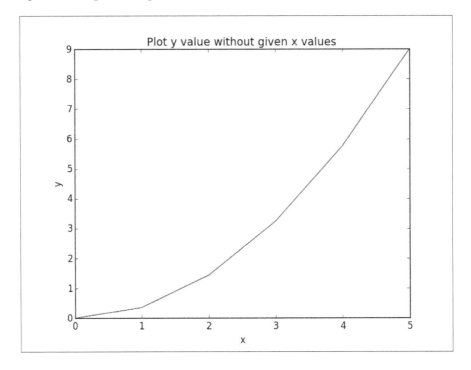

By default, the range of the axes is constrained by the range of the input x and y data. If we want to specify the viewport of the axes, we can use the axis() method to set custom ranges. For example, in the previous visualization, we could increase the range of the x axis from [0, 5] to [0, 6], and that of the y axis from [0, 9] to [0, 10], by writing the following command:

```
>>> plt.axis([0, 6, 0, 12])
```

Line properties

The default line format when we plot data in matplotlib is a solid blue line, which is abbreviated as b-. To change this setting, we only need to add the symbol code, which includes letters as color string and symbols as line style string, to the plot function. Let us consider a plot of several lines with different format styles:

```
>>> plt.plot(x*2, 'g^', x*3, 'rs', x**x, 'y-')
>>> plt.axis([0, 6, 0, 30])
>>> plt.show()
```

The output for the preceding command is as follows:

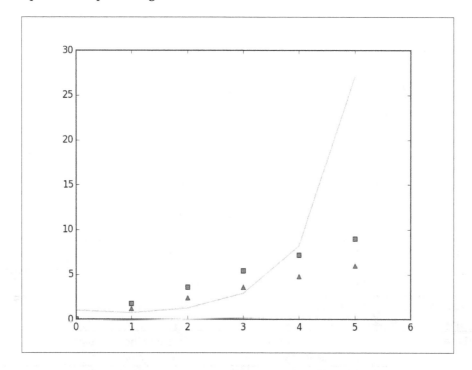

There are many line styles and attributes, such as color, line width, and dash style, that we can choose from to control the appearance of our plots. The following example illustrates several ways to set line properties:

```
>>> line = plt.plot(y, color='red', linewidth=2.0)
>>> line.set_linestyle('--')
>>> plt.setp(line, marker='o')
>>> plt.show()
```

The output for the preceding command is as follows:

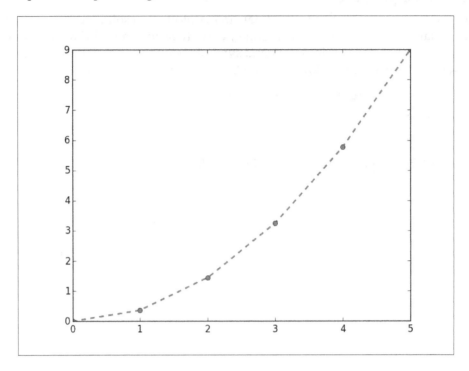

The following table lists some common properties of the line2d plotting:

Property	Value type	Description
color or c	Any matplotlib color	This sets the color of the line in the figure
dashes	On/off	This sets the sequence of ink in the points
data	np.array xdata, np.array ydata	This sets the data used for visualization
linestyle or ls	['-' | '—' | '-.' | ':' | ...]	This sets the line style in the figure
linewidth or lw	Float value in points	This sets the width of line in the figure
marker	Any symbol	This sets the style at data points in the figure

Figures and subplots

By default, all plotting commands apply to the current figure and axes. In some situations, we want to visualize data in multiple figures and axes to compare different plots or to use the space on a page more efficiently. There are two steps required before we can plot the data. Firstly, we have to define which figure we want to plot. Secondly, we need to figure out the position of our subplot in the figure:

```
>>> plt.figure('a')      # define a figure, named 'a'
>>> plt.subplot(221)     # the first position of 4 subplots in 2x2 figure
>>> plt.plot(y+y, 'r--')
>>> plt.subplot(222)     # the second position of 4 subplots
>>> plt.plot(y*3, 'ko')
>>> plt.subplot(223)     # the third position of 4 subplots
>>> plt.plot(y*y, 'b^')
>>> plt.subplot(224)
>>> plt.show()
```

The output for the preceding command is as follows:

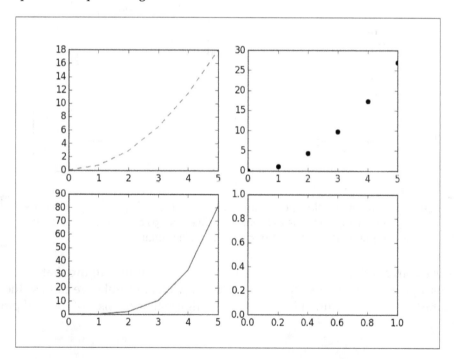

In this case, we currently have the figure a. If we want to modify any subplot in figure a, we first call the command to select the figure and subplot, and then execute the function to modify the subplot. Here, for example, we change the title of the second plot of our four-plot figure:

```
>>> plt.figure('a')
>>> plt.subplot(222)
>>> plt.title('visualization of y*3')
>>> plt.show()
```

The output for the preceding command is as follows:

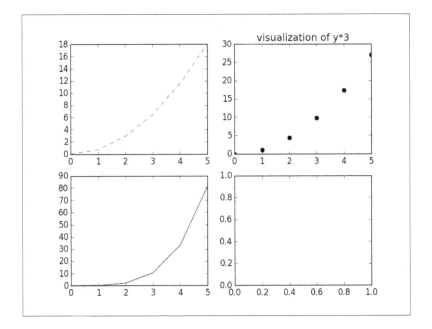

 Integer subplot specification must be a three-digit number if we are not using commas to separate indices. So, plt.subplot(221) is equal to the plt.subplot(2,2,1) command.

There is a convenience method, plt.subplots(), to creating a figure that contains a given number of subplots. As inthe previous example, we can use the plt.subplots(2,2) command to create a 2x2 figure that consists of four subplots.

We can also create the axes manually, instead of rectangular grid, by using the `plt.axes([left, bottom, width, height])` command, where all input parameters are in the fractional `[0, 1]` coordinates:

```
>>> plt.figure('b')     # create another figure, named 'b'
>>> ax1 = plt.axes([0.05, 0.1, 0.4, 0.32])
>>> ax2 = plt.axes([0.52, 0.1, 0.4, 0.32])
>>> ax3 = plt.axes([0.05, 0.53, 0.87, 0.44])
>>> plt.show()
```

The output for the preceding command is as follows:

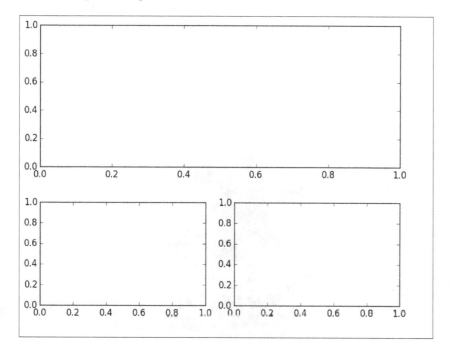

However, when you manually create axes, it takes more time to balance coordinates and sizes between subplots to arrive at a well-proportioned figure.

Exploring plot types

We have looked at how to create simple line plots so far. The matplotlib library supports many more plot types that are useful for data visualization. However, our goal is to provide the basic knowledge that will help you to understand and use the library for visualizing data in the most common situations. Therefore, we will only focus on four kinds of plot types: **scatter plots**, **bar plots**, **contour plots**, and **histograms**.

Scatter plots

A scatter plot is used to visualize the relationship between variables measured in the same dataset. It is easy to plot a simple scatter plot, using the `plt.scatter()` function, that requires numeric columns for both the x and y axis:

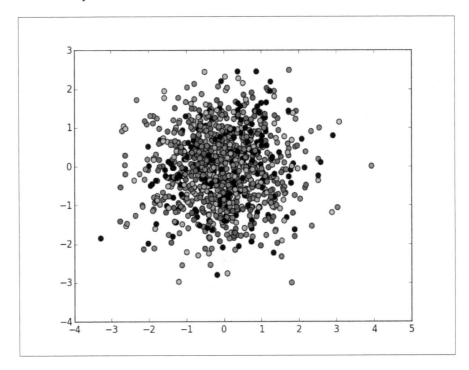

Let's take a look at the command for the preceding output:

```
>>> X = np.random.normal(0, 1, 1000)
>>> Y = np.random.normal(0, 1, 1000)
>>> plt.scatter(X, Y, c = ['b', 'g', 'k', 'r', 'c'])
>>> plt.show()
```

Bar plots

A bar plot is used to present grouped data with rectangular bars, which can be either vertical or horizontal, with the lengths of the bars corresponding to their values. We use the `plt.bar()` command to visualize a vertical bar, and the `plt.barh()` command for the other:

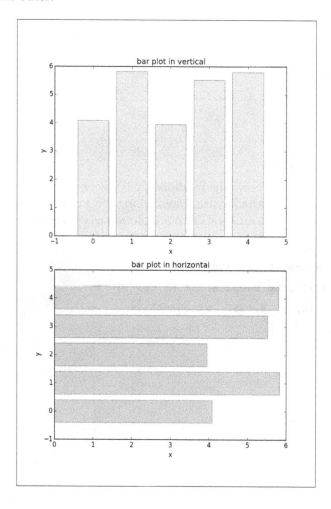

The command for the preceding output is as follows:

```
>>> X = np.arange(5)
>>> Y = 3.14 + 2.71 * np.random.rand(5)
>>> plt.subplots(2)
>>> # the first subplot
>>> plt.subplot(211)
>>> plt.bar(X, Y, align='center', alpha=0.4, color='y')
>>> plt.xlabel('x')
>>> plt.ylabel('y')
>>> plt.title('bar plot in vertical')
>>> # the second subplot
>>> plt.subplot(212)
>>> plt.barh(X, Y, align='center', alpha=0.4, color='c')
>>> plt.xlabel('x')
>>> plt.ylabel('y')
>>> plt.title('bar plot in horizontal')
>>> plt.show()
```

Contour plots

We use contour plots to present the relationship between three numeric variables in two dimensions. Two variables are drawn along the x and y axes, and the third variable, z, is used for contour levels that are plotted as curves in different colors:

```
>>> x = np.linspace(-1, 1, 255)
>>> y = np.linspace(-2, 2, 300)
>>> z = np.sin(y[:, np.newaxis]) * np.cos(x)
>>> plt.contour(x, y, z, 255, linewidth=2)
>>> plt.show()
```

Let's take a look at the contour plot in the following image:

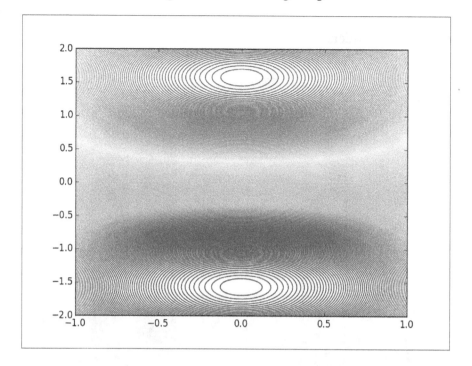

 If we want to draw contour lines and filled contours, we can use the `plt.contourf()` method instead of `plt.contour()`. In contrast to MATLAB, matplotlib's `contourf()` will not draw the polygon edges.

Histogram plots

A histogram represents the distribution of numerical data graphically. Usually, the range of values is partitioned into bins of equal size, with the height of each bin corresponding to the frequency of values within that bin:

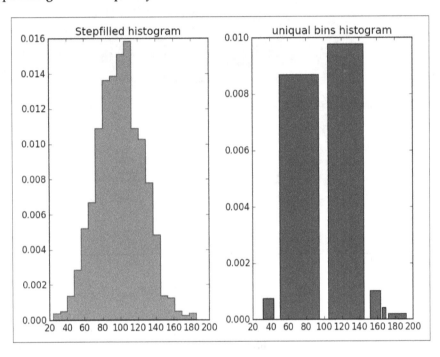

The command for the preceding output is as follows:

```
>>> mu, sigma = 100, 25
>>> fig, (ax0, ax1) = plt.subplots(ncols=2)
>>> x = mu + sigma * np.random.randn(1000)
>>> ax0.hist(x,20, normed=1, histtype='stepfilled',
                facecolor='g', alpha=0.75)
>>> ax0.set_title('Stepfilled histogram')
>>> ax1.hist(x, bins=[100,150, 165, 170, 195] normed=1,
                histtype='bar', rwidth=0.8)
>>> ax1.set_title('uniquel bins histogram')
>>> # automatically adjust subplot parameters to give specified padding
>>> plt.tight_layout()
>>> plt.show()
```

Legends and annotations

Legends are an important element that is used to identify the `plot` elements in a figure. The easiest way to show a legend inside a figure is to use the `label` argument of the `plot` function, and show the labels by calling the `plt.legend()` method:

```
>>> x = np.linspace(0, 1, 20)
>>> y1 = np.sin(x)
>>> y2 = np.cos(x)
>>> y3 = np.tan(x)
>>> plt.plot(x, y1, 'c', label='y=sin(x)')
>>> plt.plot(x, y2, 'y', label='y=cos(x)')
>>> plt.plot(x, y3, 'r', label='y=tan(x)')
>>> plt.lengend(loc='upper left')
>>> plt.show()
```

The output for the preceding command as follows:

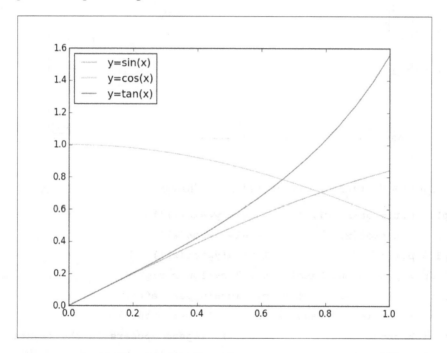

The `loc` argument in the legend command is used to figure out the position of the label box. There are several valid location options: `lower left`, `right`, `upper left`, `lower center`, `upper right`, `center`, `lower right`, `upper right`, `center right`, `best`, `upper center`, and `center left`. The default position setting is `upper right`. However, when we set an invalid location option that does not exist in the above list, the function automatically falls back to the best option.

If we want to split the legend into multiple boxes in a figure, we can manually set our expected labels for plot lines, as shown in the following image:

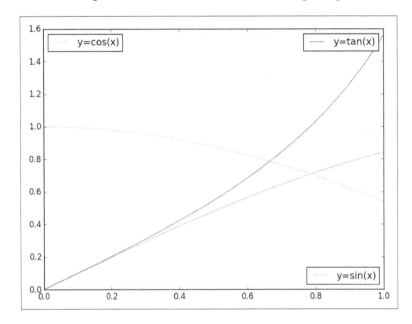

The output for the preceding command is as follows:

```
>>> p1 = plt.plot(x, y1, 'c', label='y=sin(x)')
>>> p2 = plt.plot(x, y2, 'y', label='y=cos(x)')
>>> p3 = plt.plot(x, y3, 'r', label='y=tan(x)')
>>> lsin = plt.legend(handles=p1, loc='lower right')
>>> lcos = plt.legend(handles=p2, loc='upper left')
>>> ltan = plt.legend(handles=p3, loc='upper right')
>>> # with above code, only 'y=tan(x)' legend appears in the figure
>>> # fix: add lsin, lcos as separate artists to the axes
```

```
>>> plt.gca().add_artist(lsin)
>>> plt.gca().add_artist(lcos)
>>> # automatically adjust subplot parameters to specified padding
>>> plt.tight_layout()
>>> plt.show()
```

The other element in a figure that we want to introduce is the annotations which can consist of text, arrows, or other shapes to explain parts of the figure in detail, or to emphasize some special data points. There are different methods for showing annotations, such as text, arrow, and annotation.

- The text method draws text at the given coordinates (x, y) on the plot; optionally with custom properties. There are some common arguments in the function: x, y, label text, and font-related properties that can be passed in via fontdict, such as family, fontsize, and style.

- The annotate method can draw both text and arrows arranged appropriately. Arguments of this function are s (label text), xy (the position of element to annotation), xytext (the position of the label s), xycoords (the string that indicates what type of coordinate xy is), and arrowprops (the dictionary of line properties for the arrow that connects the annotation).

Here is a simple example to illustrate the annotate and text functions:

```
>>> x = np.linspace(-2.4, 0.4, 20)
>>> y = x*x + 2*x + 1
>>> plt.plot(x, y, 'c', linewidth=2.0)
>>> plt.text(-1.5, 1.8, 'y=x^2 + 2*x + 1',
            fontsize=14, style='italic')
>>> plt.annotate('minima point', xy=(-1, 0),
            xytext=(-1, 0.3),
            horizontalalignment='center',
            verticalalignment='top',
            arrowprops=dict(arrowstyle='->',
            connectionstyle='arc3'))
>>> plt.show()
```

The output for the preceding command is as follows:

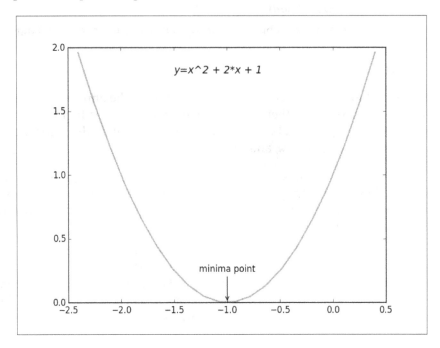

Plotting functions with Pandas

We have covered most of the important components in a plot figure using matplotlib. In this section, we will introduce another powerful plotting method for directly creating standard visualization from Pandas data objects that are often used to manipulate data.

For Series or DataFrame objects in Pandas, most plotting types are supported, such as line, bar, box, histogram, and scatter plots, and pie charts. To select a plot type, we use the `kind` argument of the `plot` function. With no kind of plot specified, the `plot` function will generate a line style visualization by default , as in the following example:

```
>>> s = pd.Series(np.random.normal(10, 8, 20))
>>> s.plot(style='ko-', alpha=0.4, label='Series plotting')
>>> plt.legend()
>>> plt.show()
```

The output for the preceding command is as follows:

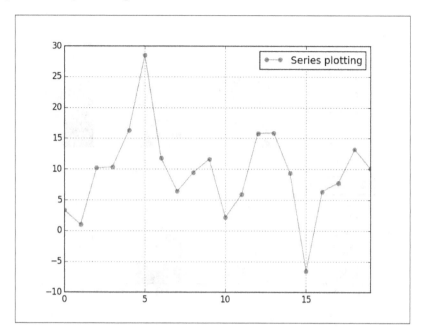

Another example will visualize the data of a DataFrame object consisting of multiple columns:

```
>>> data = {'Median_Age': [24.2, 26.4, 28.5, 30.3],
            'Density': [244, 256, 268, 279]}
>>> index_label = ['2000', '2005', '2010', '2014'];
>>> df1 = pd.DataFrame(data, index=index_label)
>>> df1.plot(kind='bar', subplots=True, sharex=True)
>>> plt.tight_layout();
>>> plt.show()
```

The output for the preceding command is as follows:

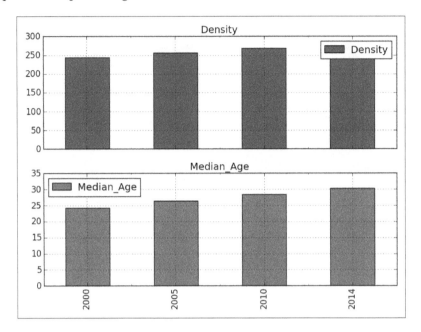

The plot method of the DataFrame has a number of options that allow us to handle the plotting of the columns. For example, in the above DataFrame visualization, we chose to plot the columns in separate subplots. The following table lists more options:

Argument	Value	Description
subplots	True/False	The plots each data column in a separate subplot
logy	True/False	The gets a log-scale y axis
secondary_y	True/False	The plots data on a secondary y axis
sharex, sharey	True/False	The shares the same x or y axis, linking sticks and limits

Additional Python data visualization tools

Besides matplotlib, there are other powerful data visualization toolkits based on Python. While we cannot dive deeper into these libraries, we would like to at least briefly introduce them in this session.

Bokeh

Bokeh is a project by Peter Wang, Hugo Shi, and others at Continuum Analytics. It aims to provide elegant and engaging visualizations in the style of D3.js. The library can quickly and easily create interactive plots, dashboards, and data applications. Here are a few differences between matplotlib and Bokeh:

- Bokeh achieves cross-platform ubiquity through IPython's new model of in-browser client-side rendering

- Bokeh uses a syntax familiar to R and ggplot users, while matplotlib is more familiar to Matlab users

- Bokeh has a coherent vision to build a ggplot-inspired in-browser interactive visualization tool, while Matplotlib has a coherent vision of focusing on 2D cross-platform graphics.

The basic steps for creating plots with Bokeh are as follows:

- Prepare some data in a list, series, and Dataframe

- Tell Bokeh where you want to generate the output

- Call `figure()` to create a plot with some overall options, similar to the matplotlib options discussed earlier

- Add renderers for your data, with visual customizations such as colors, legends, and width

- Ask Bokeh to `show()` or `save()` the results

MayaVi

MayaVi is a library for interactive scientific data visualization and 3D plotting, built on top of the award-winning **visualization toolkit** (**VTK**), which is a traits-based wrapper for the open-source visualization library. It offers the following:

- The possibility to interact with the data and object in the visualization through dialogs.

- An interface in Python for scripting. MayaVi can work with Numpy and scipy for 3D plotting out of the box and can be used within IPython notebooks, which is similar to matplotlib.

- An abstraction over VTK that offers a simpler programming model.

Let's view an illustration made entirely using MayaVi based on VTK examples and their provided data:

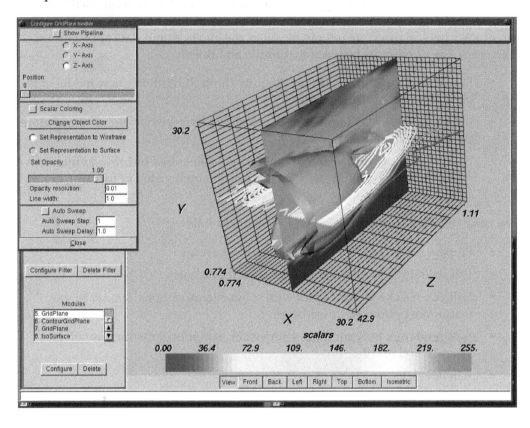

Summary

We finished covering most of the basics, such as functions, arguments, and properties for data visualization, based on the matplotlib library. We hope that, through the examples, you will be able to understand and apply them to your own problems. In general, to visualize data, we need to consider five steps- that is, getting data into suitable Python or Pandas data structures, such as lists, dictionaries, Series, or DataFrames. We explained in the previous chapters, how to accomplish this step. The second step is defining plots and subplots for the data object in question. We discussed this in the figures and subplots session. The third step is selecting a plot style and its attributes to show in the subplots such as: `line`, `bar`, `histogram`, `scatter plot`, `line style`, and `color`. The fourth step is adding extra components to the subplots, like legends, annotations and text. The fifth step is displaying or saving the results.

By now, you can do quite a few things with a dataset; for example, manipulation, cleaning, exploration, and visualization based on Python libraries such as Numpy, Pandas, and matplotlib. You can now combine this knowledge and practice with these libraries to get more and more familiar with Python data analysis.

Practice exercises:

- Name two real or fictional datasets and explain which kind of plot would best fit the data: line plots, bar charts, scatter plots, contour plots, or histograms. Name one or two applications, where each of the plot type is common (for example, histograms are often used in image editing applications).

- We only focused on the most common plot types of matplotlib. After a bit of research, can you name a few more plot types that are available in matplotlib?

- Take one Pandas data structure from *Chapter 3*, *Data Analysis with Pandas* and plot the data in a suitable way. Then, save it as a PNG image to the disk.

5
Time Series

Time series typically consist of a sequence of data points coming from measurements taken over time. This kind of data is very common and occurs in a multitude of fields.

A business executive is interested in stock prices, prices of goods and services or monthly sales figures. A meteorologist takes temperature measurements several times a day and also keeps records of precipitation, humidity, wind direction and force. A neurologist can use electroencephalography to measure electrical activity of the brain along the scalp. A sociologist can use campaign contribution data to learn about political parties and their supporters and use these insights as an argumentation aid. More examples for time series data can be enumerated almost endlessly.

Time series primer

In general, time series serve two purposes. First, they help us to learn about the underlying process that generated the data. On the other hand, we would like to be able to forecast future values of the same or related series using existing data. When we measure temperature, precipitation or wind, we would like to learn more about more complex things, such as weather or the climate of a region and how various factors interact. At the same time, we might be interested in weather forecasting.

In this chapter we will explore the time series capabilities of Pandas. Apart from its powerful core data structures – the series and the DataFrame – Pandas comes with helper functions for dealing with time related data. With its extensive built-in optimizations, Pandas is capable of handling large time series with millions of data points with ease.

We will gradually approach time series, starting with the basic building blocks of date and time objects.

Working with date and time objects

Python supports date and time handling in the date time and time modules from the standard library:

```
>>> import datetime
>>> datetime.datetime(2000, 1, 1)
datetime.datetime(2000, 1, 1, 0, 0)
```

Sometimes, dates are given or expected as strings, so a conversion from or to strings is necessary, which is realized by two functions: strptime and strftime, respectively:

```
>>> datetime.datetime.strptime("2000/1/1", "%Y/%m/%d")
datetime.datetime(2000, 1, 1, 0, 0)
>>> datetime.datetime(2000, 1, 1, 0, 0).strftime("%Y%m%d")
'20000101'
```

Real-world data usually comes in all kinds of shapes and it would be great if we did not need to remember the exact date format specifies for parsing. Thankfully, Pandas abstracts away a lot of the friction, when dealing with strings representing dates or time. One of these helper functions is to_datetime:

```
>>> import pandas as pd
>>> import numpy as np
>>> pd.to_datetime("4th of July")
Timestamp('2015-07-04
>>> pd.to_datetime("13.01.2000")
Timestamp('2000-01-13 00:00:00')
>>> pd.to_datetime("7/8/2000")
Timestamp('2000-07-08 00:00:00')
```

The last can refer to August 7th or July 8th, depending on the region. To disambiguate this case, to_datetime can be passed a keyword argument dayfirst:

```
>>> pd.to_datetime("7/8/2000", dayfirst=True)
Timestamp('2000-08-07 00:00:00')
```

Timestamp objects can be seen as Pandas' version of datetime objects and indeed, the Timestamp class is a subclass of datetime:

```
>>> issubclass(pd.Timestamp, datetime.datetime)
True
```

Which means they can be used interchangeably in many cases:

```
>>> ts = pd.to_datetime(946684800000000000)
>>> ts.year, ts.month, ts.day, ts.weekday()
(2000, 1, 1, 5)
```

Timestamp objects are an important part of time series capabilities of Pandas, since timestamps are the building block of `DateTimeIndex` objects:

```
>>> index = [pd.Timestamp("2000-01-01"),
             pd.Timestamp("2000-01-02"),
             pd.Timestamp("2000-01-03")]
>>> ts = pd.Series(np.random.randn(len(index)), index=index)
>>> ts
2000-01-01    0.731897
2000-01-02    0.761540
2000-01-03   -1.316866
dtype: float64
>>> ts.indexDatetime
Index(['2000-01-01', '2000-01-02', '2000-01-03'],
dtype='datetime64[ns]', freq=None, tz=None)
```

There are a few things to note here: We create a list of timestamp objects and pass it to the series constructor as index. This list of timestamps gets converted into a `DatetimeIndex` on the fly. If we had passed only the date strings, we would not get a `DatetimeIndex`, just an `index`:

```
>>> ts = pd.Series(np.random.randn(len(index)), index=[
             "2000-01-01", "2000-01-02", "2000-01-03"])
>>> ts.index
Index([u'2000-01-01', u'2000-01-02', u'2000-01-03'], dtype='object')
```

However, the `to_datetime` function is flexible enough to be of help, if all we have is a list of date strings:

```
>>> index = pd.to_datetime(["2000-01-01", "2000-01-02", "2000-01-03"])
>>> ts = pd.Series(np.random.randn(len(index)), index=index)
>>> ts.index
DatetimeIndex(['2000-01-01', '2000-01-02', '2000-01-03'],
dtype='datetime64[ns]', freq=None, tz=None))
```

Another thing to note is that while we have a `DatetimeIndex`, the `freq` and `tz` attributes are both `None`. We will learn about the utility of both attributes later in this chapter.

With `to_datetime` we are able to convert a variety of strings and even lists of strings into timestamp or `DatetimeIndex` objects. Sometimes we are not explicitly given all the information about a series and we have to generate sequences of time stamps of fixed intervals ourselves.

Pandas offer another great utility function for this task: `date_range`.

The `date_range` function helps to generate a fixed frequency `datetime` index between start and end dates. It is also possible to specify either the start or end date and the number of timestamps to generate.

The frequency can be specified by the `freq` parameter, which supports a number of offsets. You can use typical time intervals like hours, minutes, and seconds:

```
>>> pd.date_range(start="2000-01-01", periods=3, freq='H')
DatetimeIndex(['2000-01-01 00:00:00', '2000-01-01 01:00:00',
   '2000-01-01 02:00:00'], dtype='datetime64[ns]', freq='H', tz=None)
>>> pd.date_range(start="2000-01-01", periods=3, freq='T')
DatetimeIndex(['2000-01-01 00:00:00', '2000-01-01 00:01:00',
   '2000-01-01 00:02:00'], dtype='datetime64[ns]', freq='T', tz=None)

>>> pd.date_range(start="2000-01-01", periods=3, freq='S')
DatetimeIndex(['2000-01-01 00:00:00', '2000-01-01 00:00:01',
   '2000-01-01 00:00:02'], dtype='datetime64[ns]', freq='S', tz=None)
```

The `freq` attribute allows us to specify a multitude of options. Pandas has been used successfully in finance and economics, not least because it is really simple to work with business dates as well. As an example, to get an index with the first three business days of the millennium, the B offset alias can be used:

```
>>> pd.date_range(start="2000-01-01", periods=3, freq='B')
DatetimeIndex(['2000-01-03', '2000-01-04', '2000-01-05'],
dtype='datetime64[ns]', freq='B', tz=None)
```

The following table shows the available offset aliases and can be also be looked up in the Pandas documentation on time series under `http://pandas.pydata.org/pandas-docs/stable/timeseries.html#offset-aliases`:

Alias	Description
B	Business day frequency
C	Custom business day frequency
D	Calendar day frequency
W	Weekly frequency

Alias	Description
M	Month end frequency
BM	Business month end frequency
CBM	Custom business month end frequency
MS	Month start frequency
BMS	Business month start frequency
CBMS	Custom business month start frequency
Q	Quarter end frequency
BQ	Business quarter frequency
QS	Quarter start frequency
BQS	Business quarter start frequency
A	Year end frequency
BA	Business year end frequency
AS	Year start frequency
BAS	Business year start frequency
BH	Business hour frequency
H	Hourly frequency
T	Minutely frequency
S	Secondly frequency
L	Milliseconds
U	Microseconds
N	Nanoseconds

Moreover, The offset aliases can be used in combination as well. Here, we are generating a `datetime` index with five elements, each one day, one hour, one minute and one second apart:

```
>>> pd.date_range(start="2000-01-01", periods=5, freq='1D1h1min10s')
DatetimeIndex(['2000-01-01 00:00:00', '2000-01-02 01:01:10',
               '2000-01-03 02:02:20', '2000-01-04 03:03:30',
               '2000-01-05 04:04:40'],
              dtype='datetime64[ns]', freq='90070S', tz=None)
```

If we want to index data every 12 hours of our business time, which by default starts at 9 AM and ends at 5 PM, we would simply prefix the BH alias:

```
>>> pd.date_range(start="2000-01-01", periods=5, freq='12BH')
DatetimeIndex(['2000-01-03 09:00:00', '2000-01-04 13:00:00',
               '2000-01-06 09:00:00', '2000-01-07 13:00:00',
               '2000-01-11 09:00:00'],
              dtype='datetime64[ns]', freq='12BH', tz=None)
```

A custom definition of what a business hour means is also possible:

```
>>> ts.index
DatetimeIndex(['2000-01-01', '2000-01-02', '2000-01-03'],
dtype='datetime64[ns]', freq=None, tz=None)
```

We can use this custom business hour to build indexes as well:

```
>>> pd.date_range(start="2000-01-01", periods=5, freq=12 * bh)
DatetimeIndex(['2000-01-03 07:00:00', '2000-01-03 19:00:00',
               '2000-01-04 07:00:00', '2000-01-04 19:00:00',
               '2000-01-05 07:00:00', '2000-01-05 19:00:00',
               '2000-01-06 07:00:00'],
              dtype='datetime64[ns]', freq='12BH', tz=None)
```

Some frequencies allow us to specify an anchoring suffix, which allows us to express intervals, such as every Friday or every second Tuesday of the month:

```
>>> pd.date_range(start="2000-01-01", periods=5, freq='W-FRI')
DatetimeIndex(['2000-01-07', '2000-01-14', '2000-01-21', '2000-01-28',
'2000-02-04'], dtype='datetime64[ns]', freq='W-FRI', tz=None)
>>> pd.date_range(start="2000-01-01", periods=5, freq='WOM-2TUE')
DatetimeIndex(['2000-01-11', '2000-02-08', '2000-03-14', '2000-04-11',
'2000-05-09'], dtype='datetime64[ns]', freq='WOM-2TUE', tz=None)
```

Finally, we can merge various indexes of different frequencies. The possibilities are endless. We only show one example, where we combine two indexes – each over a decade – one pointing to every first business day of a year and one to the last day of February:

```
>>> s = pd.date_range(start="2000-01-01", periods=10, freq='BAS-JAN')
>>> t = pd.date_range(start="2000-01-01", periods=10, freq='A-FEB')
>>> s.union(t)
```

```
DatetimeIndex(['2000-01-03', '2000-02-29', '2001-01-01', '2001-02-28',
               '2002-01-01', '2002-02-28', '2003-01-01', '2003-02-28',
               '2004-01-01', '2004-02-29', '2005-01-03', '2005-02-28',
               '2006-01-02', '2006-02-28', '2007-01-01', '2007-02-28',
               '2008-01-01', '2008-02-29', '2009-01-01', '2009-02-28'],
              dtype='datetime64[ns]', freq=None, tz=None)
```

We see, that 2000 and 2005 did not start on a weekday and that 2000, 2004, and 2008 were the leap years.

We have seen two powerful functions so far, to_datetime and date_range. Now we want to dive into time series by first showing how you can create and plot time series data with only a few lines. In the rest of this section, we will show various ways to access and slice time series data.

It is easy to get started with time series data in Pandas. A random walk can be created and plotted in a few lines:

```
>>> index = pd.date_range(start='2000-01-01', periods=200, freq='B')
>>> ts = pd.Series(np.random.randn(len(index)), index=index)
>>> walk = ts.cumsum()
>>> walk.plot()
```

A possible output of this plot is show in the following figure:

Just as with usual series objects, you can select parts and slice the index:

```
>>> ts.head()
2000-01-03    1.464142
2000-01-04    0.103077
2000-01-05    0.762656
2000-01-06    1.157041
2000-01-07   -0.427284
Freq: B, dtype: float64
>>> ts[0]
1.4641415817112928
>>> ts[1:3]
2000-01-04    0.103077
2000-01-05    0.762656
```

We can use date strings as keys, even though our series has a `DatetimeIndex`:

```
>>> ts['2000-01-03']
1.4641415817112928
```

Even though the `DatetimeIndex` is made of timestamp objects, we can use `datetime` objects as keys as well:

```
>>> ts[datetime.datetime(2000, 1, 3)]
1.4641415817112928
```

Access is similar to lookup in dictionaries or lists, but more powerful. We can, for example, slice with strings or even mixed objects:

```
>>> ts['2000-01-03':'2000-01-05']
2000-01-03    1.464142
2000-01-04    0.103077
2000-01-05    0.762656
Freq: B, dtype: float64
>>> ts['2000-01-03':datetime.datetime(2000, 1, 5)]
2000-01-03    1.464142
2000-01-04    0.103077
2000-01-05    0.762656
Freq: B, dtype: float64
>>> ts['2000-01-03':datetime.date(2000, 1, 5)]
2000-01-03   -0.807669
2000-01-04    0.029802
2000-01-05   -0.434855
Freq: B, dtype: float64
```

It is even possible to use partial strings to select groups of entries. If we are only interested in February, we could simply write:

```
>>> ts['2000-02']
2000-02-01     0.277544
2000-02-02    -0.844352
2000-02-03    -1.900688
2000-02-04    -0.120010
2000-02-07    -0.465916
2000-02-08    -0.575722
2000-02-09     0.426153
2000-02-10     0.720124
2000-02-11     0.213050
2000-02-14    -0.604096
2000-02-15    -1.275345
2000-02-16    -0.708486
2000-02-17    -0.262574
2000-02-18     1.898234
2000-02-21     0.772746
2000-02-22     1.142317
2000-02-23    -1.461767
2000-02-24    -2.746059
2000-02-25    -0.608201
2000-02-28     0.513832
2000-02-29    -0.132000
```

To see all entries from March until May, including:

```
>>> ts['2000-03':'2000-05']
2000-03-01     0.528070
2000-03-02     0.200661
                  ...
2000-05-30     1.206963
2000-05-31     0.230351
Freq: B, dtype: float64
```

Time series can be shifted forward or backward in time. The index stays in place, the values move:

```
>>> small_ts = ts['2000-02-01':'2000-02-05']
>>> small_ts
2000-02-01     0.277544
2000-02-02    -0.844352
2000-02-03    -1.900688
2000-02-04    -0.120010
Freq: B, dtype: float64
```

```
>>> small_ts.shift(2)
2000-02-01          NaN
2000-02-02          NaN
2000-02-03     0.277544
2000-02-04    -0.844352
Freq: B, dtype: float64
```

To shift backwards in time, we simply use negative values:

```
>>> small_ts.shift(-2)
2000-02-01    -1.900688
2000-02-02    -0.120010
2000-02-03          NaN
2000-02-04          NaN
Freq: B, dtype: float64
```

Resampling time series

Resampling describes the process of frequency conversion over time series data. It is a helpful technique in various circumstances as it fosters understanding by grouping together and aggregating data. It is possible to create a new time series from daily temperature data that shows the average temperature per week or month. On the other hand, real-world data may not be taken in uniform intervals and it is required to map observations into uniform intervals or to fill in missing values for certain points in time. These are two of the main use directions of resampling: binning and aggregation, and filling in missing data. Downsampling and upsampling occur in other fields as well, such as digital signal processing. There, the process of downsampling is often called decimation and performs a reduction of the sample rate. The inverse process is called **interpolation**, where the sample rate is increased. We will look at both directions from a data analysis angle.

Downsampling time series data

Downsampling reduces the number of samples in the data. During this reduction, we are able to apply aggregations over data points. Let's imagine a busy airport with thousands of people passing through every hour. The airport administration has installed a visitor counter in the main area, to get an impression of exactly how busy their airport is.

They are receiving data from the counter device every minute. Here are the hypothetical measurements for a day, beginning at 08:00, ending 600 minutes later at 18:00:

```
>>> rng = pd.date_range('4/29/2015 8:00', periods=600, freq='T')
>>> ts = pd.Series(np.random.randint(0, 100, len(rng)), index=rng)
>>> ts.head()
2015-04-29 08:00:00     9
2015-04-29 08:01:00    60
2015-04-29 08:02:00    65
2015-04-29 08:03:00    25
2015-04-29 08:04:00    19
```

To get a better picture of the day, we can downsample this time series to larger intervals, for example, 10 minutes. We can choose an aggregation function as well. The default aggregation is to take all the values and calculate the mean:

```
>>> ts.resample('10min').head()
2015-04-29 08:00:00    49.1
2015-04-29 08:10:00    56.0
2015-04-29 08:20:00    42.0
2015-04-29 08:30:00    51.9
2015-04-29 08:40:00    59.0
Freq: 10T, dtype: float64
```

In our airport example, we are also interested in the sum of the values, that is, the combined number of visitors for a given time frame. We can choose the aggregation function by passing a function or a function name to the how parameter works:

```
>>> ts.resample('10min', how='sum').head()
2015-04-29 08:00:00    442
2015-04-29 08:10:00    409
2015-04-29 08:20:00    532
2015-04-29 08:30:00    433
2015-04-29 08:40:00    470
Freq: 10T, dtype: int64
```

Or we can reduce the sampling interval even more by resampling to an hourly interval:

```
>>> ts.resample('1h', how='sum').head()
2015-04-29 08:00:00    2745
2015-04-29 09:00:00    2897
2015-04-29 10:00:00    3088
2015-04-29 11:00:00    2616
2015-04-29 12:00:00    2691
Freq: H, dtype: int64
```

We can ask for other things as well. For example, what was the maximum number of people that passed through our airport within one hour:

```
>>> ts.resample('1h', how='max').head()
2015-04-29 08:00:00    97
2015-04-29 09:00:00    98
2015-04-29 10:00:00    99
2015-04-29 11:00:00    98
2015-04-29 12:00:00    99
Freq: H, dtype: int64
```

Or we can define a custom function if we are interested in more unusual metrics. For example, we could be interested in selecting a random sample for each hour:

```
>>> import random
>>> ts.resample('1h', how=lambda m: random.choice(m)).head()
2015-04-29 08:00:00    28
2015-04-29 09:00:00    14
2015-04-29 10:00:00    68
2015-04-29 11:00:00    31
2015-04-29 12:00:00     5
```

If you specify a function by string, Pandas uses highly optimized versions.

The built-in functions that can be used as argument to how are: sum, mean, std, sem, max, min, median, first, last, ohlc. The ohlc metric is popular in finance. It stands for open-high-low-close. An OHLC chart is a typical way to illustrate movements in the price of a financial instrument over time.

While in our airport this metric might not be that valuable, we can compute it nonetheless:

```
>>> ts.resample('1h', how='ohlc').head()
                     open  high  low  close
2015-04-29 08:00:00     9    97    0     14
2015-04-29 09:00:00    68    98    3     12
2015-04-29 10:00:00    71    99    1      1
2015-04-29 11:00:00    59    98    0      4
2015-04-29 12:00:00    56    99    3     55
```

Upsampling time series data

In upsampling, the frequency of the time series is increased. As a result, we have more sample points than data points. One of the main questions is how to account for the entries in the series where we have no measurement.

Let's start with hourly data for a single day:

```
>>> rng = pd.date_range('4/29/2015 8:00', periods=10, freq='H')
>>> ts = pd.Series(np.random.randint(0, 100, len(rng)), index=rng)
>>> ts.head()
2015-04-29 08:00:00    30
2015-04-29 09:00:00    27
2015-04-29 10:00:00    54
2015-04-29 11:00:00     9
2015-04-29 12:00:00    48
Freq: H, dtype: int64
```

If we upsample to data points taken every 15 minutes, our time series will be extended with NaN values:

```
>>> ts.resample('15min')
>>> ts.head()
2015-04-29 08:00:00     30
2015-04-29 08:15:00    NaN
2015-04-29 08:30:00    NaN
2015-04-29 08:45:00    NaN
2015-04-29 09:00:00     27
```

There are various ways to deal with missing values, which can be controlled by the fill_method keyword argument to resample. Values can be filled either forward or backward:

```
>>> ts.resample('15min', fill_method='ffill').head()
2015-04-29 08:00:00    30
2015-04-29 08:15:00    30
2015-04-29 08:30:00    30
2015-04-29 08:45:00    30
2015-04-29 09:00:00    27
Freq: 15T, dtype: int64
>>> ts.resample('15min', fill_method='bfill').head()
2015-04-29 08:00:00    30
2015-04-29 08:15:00    27
2015-04-29 08:30:00    27
2015-04-29 08:45:00    27
2015-04-29 09:00:00    27
```

With the `limit` parameter, it is possible to control the number of missing values to be filled:

```
>>> ts.resample('15min', fill_method='ffill', limit=2).head()
2015-04-29 08:00:00    30
2015-04-29 08:15:00    30
2015-04-29 08:30:00    30
2015-04-29 08:45:00    NaN
2015-04-29 09:00:00    27
Freq: 15T, dtype: float64
```

If you want to adjust the labels during resampling, you can use the `loffset` keyword argument:

```
>>> ts.resample('15min', fill_method='ffill', limit=2, loffset='5min').
head()
2015-04-29 08:05:00    30
2015-04-29 08:20:00    30
2015-04-29 08:35:00    30
2015-04-29 08:50:00    NaN
2015-04-29 09:05:00    27
Freq: 15T, dtype: float64
```

There is another way to fill in missing values. We could employ an algorithm to construct new data points that would somehow fit the existing points, for some definition of somehow. This process is called interpolation.

We can ask Pandas to interpolate a time series for us:

```
>>> tsx = ts.resample('15min')
```

```
>>> tsx.interpolate().head()
2015-04-29 08:00:00    30.00
2015-04-29 08:15:00    29.25
2015-04-29 08:30:00    28.50
2015-04-29 08:45:00    27.75
2015-04-29 09:00:00    27.00
Freq: 15T, dtype: float64
```

We saw the default `interpolate` method – a linear interpolation – in action. Pandas assumes a linear relationship between two existing points.

Pandas supports over a dozen `interpolation` functions, some of which require the `scipy` library to be installed. We will not cover `interpolation` methods in this chapter, but we encourage you to explore the various methods yourself. The right `interpolation` method will depend on the requirements of your application.

Time zone handling

While, by default, Pandas objects are time zone unaware, many real-world applications will make use of time zones. As with working with time in general, time zones are no trivial matter: do you know which countries have daylight saving time and do you know when the time zone is switched in those countries? Thankfully, Pandas builds on the time zone capabilities of two popular and proven utility libraries for time and date handling: `pytz` and `dateutil`:

```
>>> t = pd.Timestamp('2000-01-01')
>>> t.tz is None
True
```

To supply time zone information, you can use the `tz` keyword argument:

```
>>> t = pd.Timestamp('2000-01-01', tz='Europe/Berlin')
>>> t.tz
<DstTzInfo 'Europe/Berlin' CET+1:00:00 STD>
```

This works for ranges as well:

```
>>> rng = pd.date_range('1/1/2000 00:00', periods=10, freq='D',
tz='Europe/London')
>>> rng
DatetimeIndex(['2000-01-01', '2000-01-02', '2000-01-03', '2000-01-04',
               '2000-01-05', '2000-01-06', '2000-01-07', '2000-01-08',
               '2000-01-09', '2000-01-10'],
              dtype='datetime64[ns]', freq='D', tz='Europe/London')
```

Time zone objects can also be constructed beforehand:

```
>>> import pytz
>>> tz = pytz.timezone('Europe/London')
>>> rng = pd.date_range('1/1/2000 00:00', periods=10, freq='D', tz=tz)
>>> rng
DatetimeIndex(['2000-01-01', '2000-01-02', '2000-01-03', '2000-01-04',
               '2000-01-05', '2000-01-06', '2000-01-07', '2000-01-08',
               '2000-01-09', '2000-01-10'],
              dtype='datetime64[ns]', freq='D', tz='Europe/London')
```

Sometimes, you will already have a time zone unaware time series object that you would like to make time zone aware. The `tz_localize` function helps to switch between time zone aware and time zone unaware objects:

```
>>> rng = pd.date_range('1/1/2000 00:00', periods=10, freq='D')
>>> ts = pd.Series(np.random.randn(len(rng)), rng)
>>> ts.index.tz is None
True
>>> ts_utc = ts.tz_localize('UTC')
>>> ts_utc.index.tz
<UTC>
```

To move a time zone aware object to other time zones, you can use the `tz_convert` method:

```
>>> ts_utc.tz_convert('Europe/Berlin').index.tz
<DstTzInfo 'Europe/Berlin' LMT+0:53:00 STD>
```

Finally, to detach any time zone information from an object, it is possible to pass `None` to either `tz_convert` or `tz_localize`:

```
>>> ts_utc.tz_convert(None).index.tz is None
True
>>> ts_utc.tz_localize(None).index.tz is None
True
```

Timedeltas

Along with the powerful timestamp object, which acts as a building block for the `DatetimeIndex`, there is another useful data structure, which has been introduced in Pandas 0.15 – the Timedelta. The Timedelta can serve as a basis for indices as well, in this case a `TimedeltaIndex`.

Timedeltas are differences in times, expressed in difference units. The `Timedelta` class in Pandas is a subclass of `datetime.timedelta` from the Python standard library. As with other Pandas data structures, the Timedelta can be constructed from a variety of inputs:

```
>>> pd.Timedelta('1 days')
Timedelta('1 days 00:00:00')
>>> pd.Timedelta('-1 days 2 min 10s 3us')
```

```
Timedelta('-2 days +23:57:49.999997')
>>> pd.Timedelta(days=1,seconds=1)
Timedelta('1 days 00:00:01')
```

As you would expect, `Timedeltas` allow basic arithmetic:

```
>>> pd.Timedelta(days=1) + pd.Timedelta(seconds=1)
Timedelta('1 days 00:00:01')
```

Similar to `to_datetime`, there is a `to_timedelta` function that can parse strings or lists of strings into Timedelta structures or `TimedeltaIndices`:

```
>>> pd.to_timedelta('20.1s')
Timedelta('0 days 00:00:20.100000')
```

Instead of absolute dates, we could create an index of `timedeltas`. Imagine measurements from a volcano, for example. We might want to take measurements but index it from a given date, for example the date of the last eruption. We could create a `timedelta` index that has the last seven days as entries:

```
>>> pd.to_timedelta(np.arange(7), unit='D')
TimedeltaIndex(['0 days', '1 days', '2 days', '3 days', '4 days', '5
days', '6 days'], dtype='timedelta64[ns]', freq=None)
```

We could then work with time series data, indexed from the last eruption. If we had measurements for many eruptions (from possibly multiple volcanos), we would have an index that would make comparisons and analysis of this data easier. For example, we could ask whether there is a typical pattern that occurs between the third day and the fifth day after an eruption. This question would not be impossible to answer with a `DatetimeIndex`, but a `TimedeltaIndex` makes this kind of exploration much more convenient.

Time series plotting

Pandas comes with great support for plotting, and this holds true for time series data as well.

As a first example, let's take some monthly data and plot it:

```
>>> rng = pd.date_range(start='2000', periods=120, freq='MS')
>>> ts = pd.Series(np.random.randint(-10, 10, size=len(rng)), rng).
cumsum()
>>> ts.head()
```

```
2000-01-01    -4
2000-02-01    -6
2000-03-01   -16
2000-04-01   -26
2000-05-01   -24
Freq: MS, dtype: int64
```

Since matplotlib is used under the hood, we can pass a familiar parameter to plot, such as c for color, or title for the chart title:

```
>>> ts.plot(c='k', title='Example time series')
>>> plt.show()
```

The following figure shows an example time series plot:

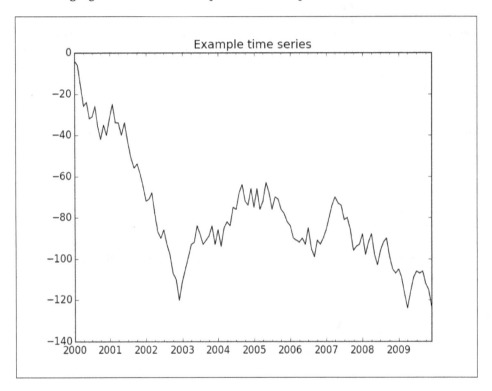

We can overlay an aggregate plot over 2 and 5 years:

```
>>> ts.resample('2A').plot(c='0.75', ls='--')
>>> ts.resample('5A').plot(c='0.25', ls='-.')
```

The following figure shows the resampled 2-year plot:

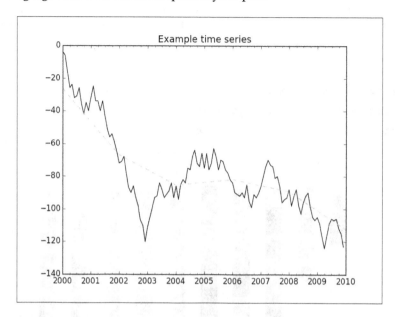

The following figure shows the resample 5-year plot:

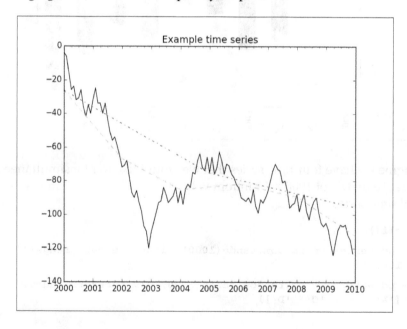

We can pass the kind of chart to the `plot` method as well. The return value of the `plot` method is an `AxesSubplot`, which allows us to customize many aspects of the plot. Here we are setting the label values on the X axis to the year values from our time series:

```
>>> plt.clf()
>>> tsx = ts.resample('1A')
>>> ax = tsx.plot(kind='bar', color='k')
>>> ax.set_xticklabels(tsx.index.year)
```

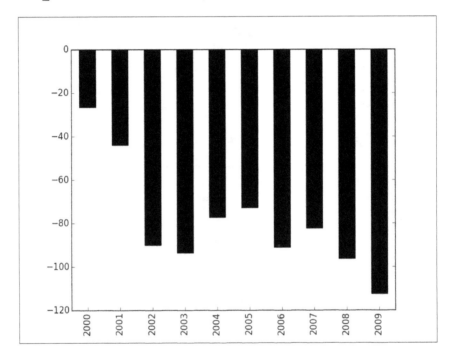

Let's imagine we have four time series that we would like to plot simultaneously. We generate a matrix of 1000 × 4 random values and treat each column as a separated time series:

```
>>> plt.clf()
>>> ts = pd.Series(np.random.randn(1000), index=pd.date_range('1/1/2000',
periods=1000))
>>> df = pd.DataFrame(np.random.randn(1000, 4), index=ts.index,
columns=['A', 'B', 'C', 'D'])
```

```
>>> df = df.cumsum()
>>> df.plot(color=['k', '0.75', '0.5', '0.25'], ls='--')
```

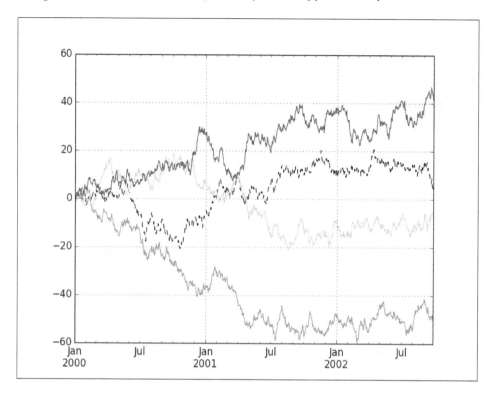

Summary

In this chapter we showed how you can work with time series in Pandas. We introduced two index types, the `DatetimeIndex` and the `TimedeltaIndex` and explored their building blocks in depth. Pandas comes with versatile helper functions that take much of the pain out of parsing dates of various formats or generating fixed frequency sequences. Resampling data can help get a more condensed picture of the data, or it can help align various datasets of different frequencies to one another. One of the explicit goals of Pandas is to make it easy to work with missing data, which is also relevant in the context of upsampling.

Finally, we showed how time series can be visualized. Since matplotlib and Pandas are natural companions, we discovered that we can reuse our previous knowledge about matplotlib for time series data as well.

In the next chapter, we will explore ways to load and store data in text files and databases.

Practice examples

Exercise 1: Find one or two real-world examples for data sets, which could – in a sensible way – be assigned to the following groups:

- Fixed frequency data
- Variable frequency data
- Data where frequency is usually measured in seconds
- Data where frequency is measured in nanoseconds
- Data, where a `TimedeltaIndex` would be preferable

Create various fixed frequency ranges:

- Every minute between 1 AM and 2 AM on 2000-01-01
- Every two hours for a whole week starting 2000-01-01
- An entry for every Saturday and Sunday during the year 2000
- An entry for every Monday of a month, if it was a business day, for the years 2000, 2001 and 2002

Interacting with Databases

6

Data analysis starts with data. It is therefore beneficial to work with data storage systems that are simple to set up, operate and where the data access does not become a problem in itself. In short, we would like to have database systems that are easy to embed into our data analysis processes and workflows. In this book, we focus mostly on the Python side of the database interaction, and we will learn how to get data into and out of Pandas data structures.

There are numerous ways to store data. In this chapter, we are going to learn to interact with three main categories: text formats, binary formats and databases. We will focus on two storage solutions, MongoDB and Redis. MongoDB is a document-oriented database, which is easy to start with, since we can store JSON documents and do not need to define a schema upfront. Redis is a popular in-memory data structure store on top of which many applications can be built. It is possible to use Redis as a fast key-value store, but Redis supports lists, sets, hashes, bit arrays and even advanced data structures such as HyperLogLog out of the box as well.

Interacting with data in text format

Text is a great medium and it's a simple way to exchange information.
The following statement is taken from a quote attributed to *Doug McIlroy*:
Write programs to handle text streams, because that is the universal interface.

In this section we will start reading and writing data from and to text files.

Reading data from text format

Normally, the raw data logs of a system are stored in multiple text files, which can accumulate a large amount of information over time. Thankfully, it is simple to interact with these kinds of files in Python.

Pandas supports a number of functions for reading data from a text file into a DataFrame object. The most simple one is the `read_csv()` function. Let's start with a small example file:

```
$ cat example_data/ex_06-01.txt
Name,age,major_id,sex,hometown
Nam,7,1,male,hcm
Mai,11,1,female,hcm
Lan,25,3,female,hn
Hung,42,3,male,tn
Nghia,26,3,male,dn
Vinh,39,3,male,vl
Hong,28,4,female,dn
```

The `cat` is the Unix shell command that can be used to print the content of a file to the screen.

In the above example file, each column is separated by comma and the first row is a header row, containing column names. To read the data file into the DataFrame object, we type the following command:

```
>>> df_ex1 = pd.read_csv('example_data/ex_06-01.txt')
>>> df_ex1
    Name  age  major_id     sex hometown
0    Nam    7         1    male      hcm
1    Mai   11         1  female      hcm
2    Lan   25         3  female       hn
3   Hung   42         3    male       tn
4  Nghia   26         3    male       dn
5   Vinh   39         3    male       vl
6   Hong   28         4  female       dn
```

We see that the `read_csv` function uses a comma as the default delimiter between columns in the text file and the first row is automatically used as a header for the columns. If we want to change this setting, we can use the `sep` parameter to change the separated symbol and set `header=None` in case the example file does not have a caption row.

See the below example:

```
$ cat example_data/ex_06-02.txt
Nam      7        1        male     hcm
Mai      11       1        female   hcm
Lan      25       3        female   hn
Hung     42       3        male     tn
Nghia    26       3        male     dn
Vinh     39       3        male     vl
Hong     28       4        female   dn


>>> df_ex2 = pd.read_csv('example_data/ex_06-02.txt',
                          sep = '\t', header=None)
>>> df_ex2
        0    1  2        3    4
0     Nam    7  1     male  hcm
1     Mai   11  1   female  hcm
2     Lan   25  3   female   hn
3    Hung   42  3     male   tn
4   Nghia   26  3     male   dn
5    Vinh   39  3     male   vl
6    Hong   28  4   female   dn
```

We can also set a specific row as the caption row by using the `header` that's equal to the index of the selected row. Similarly, when we want to use any column in the data file as the column index of DataFrame, we set `index_col` to the name or index of the column. We again use the second data file `example_data/ex_06-02.txt` to illustrate this:

```
>>> df_ex3 = pd.read_csv('example_data/ex_06-02.txt',
                          sep = '\t', header=None,
                          index_col=0)
>>> df_ex3
        1  2        3    4
0
Nam     7  1     male  hcm
Mai    11  1   female  hcm
Lan    25  3   female   hn
```

```
Hung    42  3     male    tn
Nghia   26  3     male    dn
Vinh    39  3     male    vl
Hong    28  4   female    dn
```

Apart from those parameters, we still have a lot of useful ones that can help us load data files into Pandas objects more effectively. The following table shows some common parameters:

Parameter	Value	Description
dtype	Type name or dictionary of type of columns	Sets the data type for data or columns. By default it will try to infer the most appropriate data type.
skiprows	List-like or integer	The number of lines to skip (starting from 0).
na_values	List-like or dict, default None	Values to recognize as NA/NaN. If a dict is passed, this can be set on a per-column basis.
true_values	List	A list of values to be converted to Boolean True as well.
false_values	List	A list of values to be converted to Boolean False as well.
keep_default_na	Bool, default True	If the na_values parameter is present and keep_default_na is False, the default NaN values are ignored, otherwise they are appended to
thousands	Str, default None	The thousands separator
nrows	Int, default None	Limits the number of rows to read from the file.
error_bad_lines	Boolean, default True	If set to True, a DataFrame is returned, even if an error occurred during parsing.

Besides the `read_csv()` function, we also have some other parsing functions in Pandas:

Function	Description
`read_table`	Read the general delimited file into DataFrame
`read_fwf`	Read a table of fixed-width formatted lines into DataFrame
`read_clipboard`	Read text from the clipboard and pass to `read_table`. It is useful for converting tables from web pages

In some situations, we cannot automatically parse data files from the disk using these functions. In that case, we can also open files and iterate through the reader, supported by the CSV module in the standard library:

```
$ cat example_data/ex_06-03.txt
Nam      7       1        male     hcm
Mai      11      1        female   hcm
Lan      25      3        female   hn
Hung     42      3        male     tn        single
Nghia    26      3        male     dn        single
Vinh     39      3        male     vl
Hong     28      4        female   dn

>>> import csv
>>> f = open('data/ex_06-03.txt')
>>> r = csv.reader(f, delimiter='\t')
>>> for line in r:
>>>     print(line)
['Nam', '7', '1', 'male', 'hcm']
['Mai', '11', '1', 'female', 'hcm']
['Lan', '25', '3', 'female', 'hn']
['Hung', '42', '3', 'male', 'tn', 'single']
['Nghia', '26', '3', 'male', 'dn', 'single']
['Vinh', '39', '3', 'male', 'vl']
['Hong', '28', '4', 'female', 'dn']
```

Writing data to text format

We saw how to load data from a text file into a Pandas data structure. Now, we will learn how to export data from the data object of a program to a text file. Corresponding to the read_csv() function, we also have the to_csv() function, supported by Pandas. Let's see an example below:

```
>>> df_ex3.to_csv('example_data/ex_06-02.out', sep = ';')
```

The result will look like this:

```
$ cat example_data/ex_06-02.out
0;1;2;3;4
Nam;7;1;male;hcm
Mai;11;1;female;hcm
Lan;25;3;female;hn
Hung;42;3;male;tn
Nghia;26;3;male;dn
Vinh;39;3;male;vl
Hong;28;4;female;dn
```

If we want to skip the header line or index column when writing out data into a disk file, we can set a False value to the header and index parameters:

```
>>> import sys
>>> df_ex3.to_csv(sys.stdout, sep='\t',
                  header=False, index=False)
7       1       male    hcm
11      1       female  hcm
25      3       female  hn
42      3       male    tn
26      3       male    dn
39      3       male    vl
28      4       female  dn
```

We can also write a subset of the columns of the DataFrame to the file by specifying them in the columns parameter:

```
>>> df_ex3.to_csv(sys.stdout, columns=[3,1,4],
                  header=False, sep='\t')
```

Nam	male	7	hcm
Mai	female	11	hcm
Lan	female	25	hn
Hung	male	42	tn
Nghia	male	26	dn
Vinh	male	39	vl
Hong	female	28	dn

With series objects, we can use the same function to write data into text files, with mostly the same parameters as above.

Interacting with data in binary format

We can read and write binary serialization of Python objects with the pickle module, which can be found in the standard library. Object serialization can be useful, if you work with objects that take a long time to create, like some machine learning models. By pickling such objects, subsequent access to this model can be made faster. It also allows you to distribute Python objects in a standardized way.

Pandas includes support for pickling out of the box. The relevant methods are the `read_pickle()` and `to_pickle()` functions to read and write data from and to files easily. Those methods will write data to disk in the pickle format, which is a convenient short-term storage format:

```
>>> df_ex3.to_pickle('example_data/ex_06-03.out')
>>> pd.read_pickle('example_data/ex_06-03.out')
```

	1	2	3	4
0				
Nam	7	1	male	hcm
Mai	11	1	female	hcm
Lan	25	3	female	hn
Hung	42	3	male	tn
Nghia	26	3	male	dn
Vinh	39	3	male	vl
Hong	28	4	female	dn

HDF5

HDF5 is not a database, but a data model and file format. It is suited for write-one, read-many datasets. An HDF5 file includes two kinds of objects: data sets, which are array-like collections of data, and groups, which are folder-like containers what hold data sets and other groups. There are some interfaces for interacting with HDF5 format in Python, such as h5py which uses familiar NumPy and Python constructs, such as dictionaries and NumPy array syntax. With h5py, we have high-level interface to the HDF5 API which helps us to get started. However, in this book, we will introduce another library for this kind of format called PyTables, which works well with Pandas objects:

```
>>> store = pd.HDFStore('hdf5_store.h5')
>>> store
<class 'pandas.io.pytables.HDFStore'>
File path: hdf5_store.h5
Empty
```

We created an empty HDF5 file, named `hdf5_store.h5`. Now, we can write data to the file just like adding key-value pairs to a `dict`:

```
>>> store['ex3'] = df_ex3
>>> store['name'] = df_ex2[0]
>>> store['hometown'] = df_ex3[4]
>>> store
<class 'pandas.io.pytables.HDFStore'>
File path: hdf5_store.h5
/ex3                    frame        (shape->[7,4])
/hometown               series       (shape->[1])
/name                   series       (shape->[1])
```

Objects stored in the HDF5 file can be retrieved by specifying the object keys:

```
>>> store['name']
0       Nam
1       Mai
2       Lan
3       Hung
4       Nghia
5       Vinh
6       Hong
Name: 0, dtype: object
```

Once we have finished interacting with the HDF5 file, we close it to release the file handle:

```
>>> store.close()
>>> store
<class 'pandas.io.pytables.HDFStore'>
File path: hdf5_store.h5
File is CLOSED
```

There are other supported functions that are useful for working with the HDF5 format. You should explore ,in more detail, two libraries – `pytables` and `h5py` – if you need to work with huge quantities of data.

Interacting with data in MongoDB

Many applications require more robust storage systems then text files, which is why many applications use databases to store data. There are many kinds of databases, but there are two broad categories: relational databases, which support a standard declarative language called SQL, and so called NoSQL databases, which are often able to work without a predefined schema and where a data instance is more properly described as a document, rather as a row.

MongoDB is a kind of NoSQL database that stores data as documents, which are grouped together in collections. Documents are expressed as JSON objects. It is fast and scalable in storing, and also flexible in querying, data. To use MongoDB in Python, we need to import the `pymongo` package and open a connection to the database by passing a hostname and port. We suppose that we have a MongoDB instance, running on the default host (`localhost`) and port (`27017`):

```
>>> import pymongo
>>> conn = pymongo.MongoClient(host='localhost', port=27017)
```

If we do not put any parameters into the `pymongo.MongoClient()` function, it will automatically use the default host and port.

In the next step, we will interact with databases inside the MongoDB instance. We can list all databases that are available in the instance:

```
>>> conn.database_names()
['local']
>>> lc = conn.local
>>> lc
Database(MongoClient('localhost', 27017), 'local')
```

The above snippet says that our MongoDB instance only has one database, named 'local'. If the databases and collections we point to do not exist, MongoDB will create them as necessary:

```
>>> db = conn.db
>>> db
Database(MongoClient('localhost', 27017), 'db')
```

Each database contains groups of documents, called collections. We can understand them as tables in a relational database. To list all existing collections in a database, we use collection_names() function:

```
>>> lc.collection_names()
['startup_log', 'system.indexes']
>>> db.collection_names()
[]
```

Our db database does not have any collections yet. Let's create a collection, named person, and insert data from a DataFrame object to it:

```
>>> collection = db.person
>>> collection
Collection(Database(MongoClient('localhost', 27017), 'db'), 'person')
>>> # insert df_ex2 DataFrame into created collection
>>> import json
>>> records = json.load(df_ex2.T.to_json()).values()
>>> records
dict_values([{'2': 3, '3': 'male', '1': 39, '4': 'vl', '0': 'Vinh'},
{'2': 3, '3': 'male', '1': 26, '4': 'dn', '0': 'Nghia'}, {'2': 4, '3':
'female', '1': 28, '4': 'dn', '0': 'Hong'}, {'2': 3, '3': 'female', '1':
25, '4': 'hn', '0': 'Lan'}, {'2': 3, '3': 'male', '1': 42, '4': 'tn',
'0': 'Hung'}, {'2': 1, '3':'male', '1': 7, '4': 'hcm', '0': 'Nam'}, {'2':
1, '3': 'female', '1': 11, '4': 'hcm', '0': 'Mai'}])
>>> collection.insert(records)
[ObjectId('557da218f21c761d7c176a40'),
 ObjectId('557da218f21c761d7c176a41'),
 ObjectId('557da218f21c761d7c176a42'),
 ObjectId('557da218f21c761d7c176a43'),
 ObjectId('557da218f21c761d7c176a44'),
 ObjectId('557da218f21c761d7c176a45'),
 ObjectId('557da218f21c761d7c176a46')]
```

The `df_ex2` is transposed and converted to a JSON string before loading into a dictionary. The `insert()` function receives our created dictionary from `df_ex2` and saves it to the collection.

If we want to list all data inside the collection, we can execute the following commands:

```
>>> for cur in collection.find():
>>>     print(cur)
{'4': 'vl', '2': 3, '3': 'male', '1': 39, '_id':
ObjectId('557da218f21c761d7c176

a40'), '0': 'Vinh'}
{'4': 'dn', '2': 3, '3': 'male', '1': 26, '_id':
ObjectId('557da218f21c761d7c176

a41'), '0': 'Nghia'}
{'4': 'dn', '2': 4, '3': 'female', '1': 28, '_id':
ObjectId('557da218f21c761d7c1

76a42'), '0': 'Hong'}
{'4': 'hn', '2': 3, '3': 'female', '1': 25, '_id':
ObjectId('557da218f21c761d7c1

76a43'), '0': 'Lan'}
{'4': 'tn', '2': 3, '3': 'male', '1': 42, '_id':
ObjectId('557da218f21c761d7c176

a44'), '0': 'Hung'}
{'4': 'hcm', '2': 1, '3': 'male', '1': 7, '_id':
ObjectId('557da218f21c761d7c176

a45'), '0': 'Nam'}
{'4': 'hcm', '2': 1, '3': 'female', '1': 11, '_id':
ObjectId('557da218f21c761d7c

176a46'), '0': 'Mai'}
```

If we want to query data from the created collection with some conditions, we can use the `find()` function and pass in a dictionary describing the documents we want to retrieve. The returned result is a cursor type, which supports the iterator protocol:

```
>>> cur = collection.find({'3' : 'male'})
>>> type(cur)
pymongo.cursor.Cursor
>>> result = pd.DataFrame(list(cur))
```

```
>>> result
       0    1  2      3     4                        _id
0   Vinh   39  3   male    vl  557da218f21c761d7c176a40
1  Nghia   26  3   male    dn  557da218f21c761d7c176a41
2   Hung   42  3   male    tn  557da218f21c761d7c176a44
3    Nam    7  1   male   hcm  557da218f21c761d7c176a45
```

Sometimes, we want to delete data in MongdoDB. All we need to do is to pass a query to the remove() method on the collection:

```
>>> # before removing data
>>> pd.DataFrame(list(collection.find()))
       0    1  2       3     4                        _id
0   Vinh   39  3    male    vl  557da218f21c761d7c176a40
1  Nghia   26  3    male    dn  557da218f21c761d7c176a41
2   Hong   28  4  female    dn  557da218f21c761d7c176a42
3    Lan   25  3  female    hn  557da218f21c761d7c176a43
4   Hung   42  3    male    tn  557da218f21c761d7c176a44
5    Nam    7  1    male   hcm  557da218f21c761d7c176a45
6    Mai   11  1  female   hcm  557da218f21c761d7c176a46


>>> # after removing records which have '2' column as 1 and '3' column as
'male'
>>> collection.remove({'2': 1, '3': 'male'})
{'n': 1, 'ok': 1}
>>> cur_all = collection.find();
>>> pd.DataFrame(list(cur_all))
       0    1  2       3     4                        _id
0   Vinh   39  3    male    vl  557da218f21c761d7c176a40
1  Nghia   26  3    male    dn  557da218f21c761d7c176a41
2   Hong   28  4  female    dn  557da218f21c761d7c176a42
3    Lan   25  3  female    hn  557da218f21c761d7c176a43
4   Hung   42  3    male    tn  557da218f21c761d7c176a44
5    Mai   11  1  female   hcm  557da218f21c761d7c176a46
```

We learned step by step how to insert, query and delete data in a collection. Now, we will show how to update existing data in a collection in MongoDB:

```
>>> doc = collection.find_one({'1' : 42})
>>> doc['4'] = 'hcm'
>>> collection.save(doc)
ObjectId('557da218f21c761d7c176a44')
>>> pd.DataFrame(list(collection.find()))
```

	0	1	2	3	4	_id
0	Vinh	39	3	male	vl	557da218f21c761d7c176a40
1	Nghia	26	3	male	dn	557da218f21c761d7c176a41
2	Hong	28	4	female	dn	557da218f21c761d7c176a42
3	Lan	25	3	female	hn	557da218f21c761d7c176a43
4	Hung	42	3	male	hcm	557da218f21c761d7c176a44
5	Mai	11	1	female	hcm	557da218f21c761d7c176a46

The following table shows methods that provide shortcuts to manipulate documents in MongoDB:

Update Method	Description
inc()	Increment a numeric field
set()	Set certain fields to new values
unset()	Remove a field from the document
push()	Append a value onto an array in the document
pushAll()	Append several values onto an array in the document
addToSet()	Add a value to an array, only if it does not exist
pop()	Remove the last value of an array
pull()	Remove all occurrences of a value from an array
pullAll()	Remove all occurrences of any set of values from an array
rename()	Rename a field
bit()	Update a value by bitwise operation

Interacting with data in Redis

Redis is an advanced kind of key-value store where the values can be of different types: string, list, set, sorted set or hash. Redis stores data in memory like memcached but it can be persisted on disk, unlike memcached, which has no such option. Redis supports fast reads and writes, in the order of 100,000 set or get operations per second.

To interact with Redis, we need to install the `Redis-py` module to Python, which is available on `pypi` and can be installed with `pip`:

```
$ pip install redis
```

Now, we can connect to Redis via the host and port of the DB server. We assume that we have already installed a Redis server, which is running with the default host (`localhost`) and port (`6379`) parameters:

```
>>> import redis
>>> r = redis.StrictRedis(host='127.0.0.1', port=6379)
>>> r
StrictRedis<ConnectionPool<Connection<host=localhost,port=6379,db=0>>>
```

As a first step to storing data in Redis, we need to define which kind of data structure is suitable for our requirements. In this section, we will introduce four commonly used data structures in Redis: simple value, list, set and ordered set. Though data is stored into Redis in many different data structures, each value must be associated with a key.

The simple value

This is the most basic kind of value in Redis. For every key in Redis, we also have a value that can have a data type, such as string, integer or double. Let's start with an example for setting and getting data to and from Redis:

```
>>> r.set('gender:An', 'male')
True
>>> r.get('gender:An')
b'male'
```

In this example we want to store the gender info of a person, named `An` into Redis. Our key is `gender:An` and our value is `male`. Both of them are a type of string.

The set () function receives two parameters: the key and the value. The first parameter is the key and the second parameter is value. If we want to update the value of this key, we just call the function again and change the value of the second parameter. Redis automatically updates it.

The get () function will retrieve the value of our key, which is passed as the parameter. In this case, we want to get gender information of the key gender:An.

In the second example, we show you another kind of value type, an integer:

```
>>> r.set('visited_time:An', 12)
True
>>> r.get('visited_time:An')
b'12'
>>> r.incr('visited_time:An', 1)
13
>>> r.get('visited_time:An')
b'13'
```

We saw a new function, incr (), which used to increment the value of key by a given amount. If our key does not exist, RedisDB will create the key with the given increment as the value.

List

We have a few methods for interacting with list values in Redis. The following example uses rpush () and lrange () functions to put and get list data to and from the DB:

```
>>> r.rpush('name_list', 'Tom')
1L
>>> r.rpush('name_list', 'John')
2L
>>> r.rpush('name_list', 'Mary')
3L
>>> r.rpush('name_list', 'Jan')
4L
>>> r.lrange('name_list', 0, -1)
[b'Tom', b'John', b'Mary', b'Jan']
>>> r.llen('name_list')
4
>>> r.lindex('name_list', 1)
b'John'
```

Besides the rpush() and lrange() functions we used in the example, we also want to introduce two others functions. First, the llen() function is used to get the length of our list in the Redis for a given key. The lindex() function is another way to retrieve an item of the list. We need to pass two parameters into the function: a key and an index of item in the list. The following table lists some other powerful functions in processing list data structure with Redis:

Function	Description
rpushx(name, value)	Push value onto the tail of the list name if name exists
rpop(name)	Remove and return the last item of the list name
lset(name, index, value)	Set item at the index position of the list name to input value
lpushx(name,value)	Push value on the head of the list name if name exists
lpop(name)	Remove and return the first item of the list name

Set

This data structure is also similar to the list type. However, in contrast to a list, we cannot store duplicate values in our set:

```
>>> r.sadd('country', 'USA')
1
>>> r.sadd('country', 'Italy')
1
>>> r.sadd('country', 'Singapore')
1
>>> r.sadd('country', 'Singapore')
0
>>> r.smembers('country')
{b'Italy', b'Singapore', b'USA'}
>>> r.srem('country', 'Singapore')
1
>>> r.smembers('country')
{b'Italy', b'USA'}
```

Corresponding to the list data structure, we also have a number of functions to get, set, update or delete items in the set. They are listed in the supported functions for set data structure, in the following table:

Function	Description
`sadd(name, values)`	Add value(s) to the set with key name
`scard(name)`	Return the number of element in the set with key name
`smembers(name)`	Return all members of the set with key name
`srem(name, values)`	Remove value(s) from the set with key name

Ordered set

The ordered set data structure takes an extra attribute when we add data to a set called **score**. An ordered set will use the score to determine the order of the elements in the set:

```
>>> r.zadd('person:A', 10, 'sub:Math')
1
>>> r.zadd('person:A', 7, 'sub:Bio')
1
>>> r.zadd('person:A', 8, 'sub:Chem')
1
>>> r.zrange('person:A', 0, -1)
[b'sub:Bio', b'sub:Chem', b'sub:Math']
>>> r.zrange('person:A', 0, -1, withscores=True)
[(b'sub:Bio', 7.0), (b'sub:Chem', 8.0), (b'sub:Math', 10.0)]
```

By using the `zrange(name, start, end)` function, we can get a range of values from the sorted set between the start and end score sorted in ascending order by default. If we want to change the way method of sorting, we can set the `desc` parameter to `True`. The `withscore` parameter is used in case we want to get the scores along with the return values. The return type is a list of (value, score) pairs as you can see in the above example.

See the below table for more functions available on ordered sets:

Function	Description
`zcard(name)`	Return the number of elements in the sorted set with key name
`zincrby(name, value, amount=1)`	Increment the score of value in the sorted set with key name by amount
`zrangebyscore(name, min, max, withscores=False, start=None, num=None)`	Return a range of values from the sorted set with key name with a score between min and max. If `withscores` is `true`, return the scores along with the values. If start and `num` are given, return a slice of the range
`zrank(name, value)`	Return a 0-based value indicating the rank of value in the sorted set with key name
`zrem(name, values)`	Remove member value(s) from the sorted set with key name

Summary

We finished covering the basics of interacting with data in different commonly used storage mechanisms from the simple ones, such as text files, over more structured ones, such as HDF5, to more sophisticated data storage systems, such as MongoDB and Redis. The most suitable type of storage will depend on your use case. The choice of the data storage layer technology plays an important role in the overall design of data processing systems. Sometimes, we need to combine various database systems to store our data, such as complexity of the data, performance of the system or computation requirements.

Practice exercise

- Take a data set of your choice and design storage options for it. Consider text files, HDF5, a document database, and a data structure store as possible persistent options. Also evaluate how difficult (by some metric, for examples, how many lines of code) it would be to update or delete a specific item. Which storage type is the easiest to set up? Which storage type supports the most flexible queries?

- In *Chapter 3, Data Analysis with Pandas* we saw that it is possible to create hierarchical indices with Pandas. As an example, assume that you have data on each city with more than 1 million inhabitants and that we have a two level index, so we can address individual cities, but also whole countries. How would you represent this hierarchical relationship with the various storage options presented in this chapter: text files, HDF5, MongoDB, and Redis? What do you believe would be most convenient to work with in the long run?

7
Data Analysis Application Examples

In this chapter, we want to get you acquainted with typical data preparation tasks and analysis techniques, because being fluent in preparing, grouping, and reshaping data is an important building block for successful data analysis.

While preparing data seems like a mundane task – and often it is – it is a step we cannot skip, although we can strive to simplify it by using tools such as Pandas.

Why is preparation necessary at all? Because most useful data will come from the real world and will have deficiencies, contain errors or will be fragmentary.

There are more reasons why data preparation is useful: it gets you in close contact with the raw material. Knowing your input helps you to spot potential errors early and build confidence in your results.

Here are a few data preparation scenarios:

- A client hands you three files, each containing time series data about a single geological phenomenon, but the observed data is recorded on different intervals and uses different separators

- A machine learning algorithm can only work with numeric data, but your input only contains text labels

- You are handed the raw logs of a web server of an up and coming service and your task is to make suggestions on a growth strategy, based on existing visitor behavior

Data munging

The arsenal of tools for data munging is huge, and while we will focus on Python we want to mention some useful tools as well. If they are available on your system and you expect to work a lot with data, they are worth learning.

One group of tools belongs to the UNIX tradition, which emphasizes text processing and as a consequence has, over the last four decades, developed many high-performance and battle-tested tools for dealing with text. Some common tools are: `sed`, `grep`, `awk`, `sort`, `uniq`, `tr`, `cut`, `tail`, and `head`. They do very elementary things, such as filtering out lines (`grep`) or columns (`cut`) from files, replacing text (`sed`, `tr`) or displaying only parts of files (`head`, `tail`).

We want to demonstrate the power of these tools with a single example only.

Imagine you are handed the log files of a web server and you are interested in the distribution of the IP addresses.

Each line of the log file contains an entry in the common log server format (you can download this data set from `http://ita.ee.lbl.gov/html/contrib/EPA- HTTP.html`):

```
$ cat epa-html.txt
wpbfl2-45.gate.net [29:23:56:12] "GET /Access/ HTTP/1.0" 200 2376ebaca.
icsi.net [30:00:22:20] "GET /Info.html HTTP/1.0" 200 884
```

For instance, we want to know how often certain users have visited our site.

We are interested in the first column only, since this is where the IP address or hostname can be found. After that, we need to count the number of occurrences of each host and finally display the results in a friendly way.

The `sort | uniq -c` stanza is our workhorse here: it sorts the data first and `uniq -c` will save the number of occurrences along with the value. The `sort -nr | head -15` is our formatting part; we sort numerically (`-n`) and in reverse (`-r`), and keep only the top 15 entries.

Putting it all together with pipes:

```
$ cut -d ' ' -f 1 epa-http.txt | sort | uniq -c | sort -nr | head -15
294 sandy.rtptok1.epa.gov
292 e659229.boeing.com
266 wicdgserv.wic.epa.gov
263 keyhole.es.dupont.com
248 dwilson.pr.mcs.net
176 oea4.r8stw56.epa.gov
174 macip26.nacion.co.cr
172 dcimsd23.dcimsd.epa.gov
167 www-b1.proxy.aol.com
158 piweba3y.prodigy.com
152 wictrn13.dcwictrn.epa.gov
151 nntp1.reach.com
151 inetg1.arco.com
149 canto04.nmsu.edu
146 weisman.metrokc.gov
```

With one command, we get to convert a sequential server log into an ordered list of the most common hosts that visited our site. We also see that we do not seem to have large differences in the number of visits among our top users.

There are more little helpful tools of which the following are just a tiny selection:

- `csvkit`: This is the suite of utilities for working with CSV, the king of tabular file formats
- `jq`: This is a lightweight and flexible command-line JSON processor
- `xmlstarlet`: This is a tool that supports XML queries with XPath, among other things
- `q`: This runs SQL on text files

Where the UNIX command line ends, lightweight languages take over. You might be able to get an impression from text only, but your colleagues might appreciate visual representations, such as charts or pretty graphs, generated by matplotlib, much more.

Python and its data tools ecosystem are much more versatile than the command line, but for first explorations and simple operations the effectiveness of the command line is often unbeatable.

Cleaning data

Most real-world data will have some defects and therefore will need to go through a cleaning step first. We start with a small file. Although this file contains only four rows, it will allow us to demonstrate the process up to a cleaned data set:

```
$ cat small.csv
22,6.1
41,5.7
  18,5.3*
29,NA
```

Note that this file has a few issues. The lines that contain values are all comma-separated, but we have missing (NA) and probably unclean (5.3*) values. We can load this file into a data frame, nevertheless:

```
>>> import pandas as pd
>>> df = pd.read_csv("small.csv")
>>> df
     22    6.1
0    41    5.7
1    18    5.3*
2    29    NaN
```

Pandas used the first row as header, but this is not what we want:

```
>>> df = pd.read_csv("small.csv", header=None)
>>> df
      0     1
0    22    6.1
1    41    5.7
2    18    5.3*
3    29    NaN
```

This is better, but instead of numeric values, we would like to supply our own column names:

```
>>> df = pd.read_csv("small.csv", names=["age", "height"])
>>> df
    age height
0    22    6.1
1    41    5.7
2    18    5.3*
3    29    NaN
```

The `age` column looks good, since Pandas already inferred the intended type, but the `height` cannot be parsed into numeric values yet:

```
>>> df.age.dtype
dtype('int64')
>>> df.height.dtype
dtype('O')
```

If we try to coerce the `height` column into float values, Pandas will report an exception:

```
>>> df.height.astype('float')
ValueError: invalid literal for float(): 5.3*
```

We could use whatever value is parseable as a float and throw away the rest with the `convert_objects` method:

```
>>> df.height.convert_objects(convert_numeric=True)
0      6.1
1      5.7
2      NaN
3      NaN
Name: height, dtype: float64
```

If we know in advance the undesirable characters in our data set, we can augment the `read_csv` method with a custom converter function:

```
>>> remove_stars = lambda s: s.replace("*", "")
>>> df = pd.read_csv("small.csv", names=["age", "height"],
                     converters={"height": remove_stars})
>>> df
   age height
0   22    6.1
1   41    5.7
2   18    5.3
3   29     NA
```

Now we can finally make the height column a bit more useful. We can assign it the updated version, which has the favored type:

```
>>> df.height = df.height.convert_objects(convert_numeric=True)
>>> df
     age   height
0    22      6.1
1    41      5.7
2    18      5.3
3    29      NaN
```

If we wanted to only keep the complete entries, we could drop any row that contains undefined values:

```
>>> df.dropna()
     age   height
0    22      6.1
1    41      5.7
2    18      5.3
```

We could use a default height, maybe a fixed value:

```
>>> df.fillna(5.0)
     age   height
0    22      6.1
1    41      5.7
2    18      5.3
3    29      5.0
```

On the other hand, we could also use the average of the existing values:

```
>>> df.fillna(df.height.mean())
     age   height
0    22      6.1
1    41      5.7
2    18      5.3
3    29      5.7
```

The last three data frames are complete and correct, depending on your definition of correct when dealing with missing values. Especially, the columns have the requested types and are ready for further analysis. Which of the data frames is best suited will depend on the task at hand.

Filtering

Even if we have clean and probably correct data, we might want to use only parts of it or we might want to check for outliers. An outlier is an observation point that is distant from other observations because of variability or measurement errors. In both cases, we want to reduce the number of elements in our data set to make it more relevant for further processing.

In this example, we will try to find potential outliers. We will use the Europe Brent Crude Oil Spot Price as recorded by the U.S. Energy Information Administration. The raw Excel data is available from `http://www.eia.gov/dnav/pet/hist_xls/rbrted.xls` (it can be found in the second worksheet). We cleaned the data slightly (the cleaning process is part of an exercise at the end of this chapter) and will work with the following data frame, containing 7160 entries, ranging from 1987 to 2015:

```
>>> df.head()
        date   price
0  1987-05-20  18.63
1  1987-05-21  18.45
2  1987-05-22  18.55
3  1987-05-25  18.60
4  1987-05-26  18.63
>>> df.tail()
           date   price
7155  2015-08-04  49.08
7156  2015-08-05  49.04
7157  2015-08-06  47.80
7158  2015-08-07  47.54
7159  2015-08-10  48.30
```

While many people know about oil prices – be it from the news or the filling station – let us forget anything we know about it for a minute. We could first ask for the extremes:

```
>>> df[df.price==df.price.min()]
           date  price
2937  1998-12-10    9.1
>>> df[df.price==df.price.max()]
           date   price
5373  2008-07-03  143.95
```

Another way to find potential outliers would be to ask for values that deviate most from the mean. We can use the `np.abs` function to calculate the deviation from the mean first:

```
>>> np.abs(df.price - df.price.mean())
0         26.17137
1         26.35137
...
7157       2.99863
7158       2.73863
7159       3.49863
```

We can now compare this deviation from a multiple – we choose 2.5 – of the standard deviation:

```
>>> import numpy as np
>>> df[np.abs(df.price - df.price.mean()) > 2.5 * df.price.std()]
        date      price
5354 2008-06-06   132.81
5355 2008-06-09   134.43
5356 2008-06-10   135.24
5357 2008-06-11   134.52
5358 2008-06-12   132.11
5359 2008-06-13   134.29
5360 2008-06-16   133.90
5361 2008-06-17   131.27
5363 2008-06-19   131.84
5364 2008-06-20   134.28
5365 2008-06-23   134.54
5366 2008-06-24   135.37
5367 2008-06-25   131.59
5368 2008-06-26   136.82
5369 2008-06-27   139.38
5370 2008-06-30   138.40
5371 2008-07-01   140.67
5372 2008-07-02   141.24
5373 2008-07-03   143.95
5374 2008-07-07   139.62
5375 2008-07-08   134.15
5376 2008-07-09   133.91
5377 2008-07-10   135.81
5378 2008-07-11   143.68
5379 2008-07-14   142.43
5380 2008-07-15   136.02
5381 2008-07-16   133.31
5382 2008-07-17   134.16
```

We see that those few days in summer 2008 must have been special. Sure enough, it is not difficult to find articles and essays with titles like *Causes and Consequences of the Oil Shock of 2007–08*. We have discovered a trace to these events solely by looking at the data.

We could ask the above question for each decade separately. We first make our data frame look more like a time series:

```
>>> df.index = df.date
>>> del df["date"]
>>> df.head()
            price
date
1987-05-20  18.63
1987-05-21  18.45
1987-05-22  18.55
1987-05-25  18.60
1987-05-26  18.63
```

We could filter out the eighties:

```
>>> decade = df["1980":"1989"]
>>> decade[np.abs(decade.price - decade.price.mean()) > 2.5 * decade.price.std()]
            price
date
1988-10-03  11.60
1988-10-04  11.65
1988-10-05  11.20
1988-10-06  11.30
1988-10-07  11.35
```

We observe that within the data available (1987–1989), the fall of 1988 exhibits a slight spike in the oil prices. Similarly, during the nineties, we see that we have a larger deviation, in the fall of 1990:

```
>>> decade = df["1990":"1999"]
>>> decade[np.abs(decade.price - decade.price.mean()) > 5 * decade.price.std()]
            price
date
1990-09-24  40.75
1990-09-26  40.85
1990-09-27  41.45
1990-09-28  41.00
1990-10-09  40.90
1990-10-10  40.20
1990-10-11  41.15
```

There are many more use cases for filtering data. Space and time are typical units: you might want to filter census data by state or city, or economical data by quarter. The possibilities are endless and will be driven by your project.

Merging data

The situation is common: you have multiple data sources, but in order to make statements about the content, you would rather combine them. Fortunately, Pandas' concatenation and merge functions abstract away most of the pain, when combining, joining, or aligning data. It does so in a highly optimized manner as well.

In a case where two data frames have a similar shape, it might be useful to just append one after the other. Maybe A and B are products and one data frame contains the number of items sold per product in a store:

```
>>> df1 = pd.DataFrame({'A': [1, 2, 3], 'B': [4, 5, 6]})
>>> df1
   A  B
0  1  4
1  2  5
2  3  6
>>> df2 = pd.DataFrame({'A': [4, 5, 6], 'B': [7, 8, 9]})
>>> df2
   A  B
0  4  7
1  5  8
2  6  9
>>> df1.append(df2)
   A  B
0  1  4
1  2  5
2  3  6
0  4  7
1  5  8
2  6  9
```

Sometimes, we won't care about the indices of the originating data frames:

```
>>> df1.append(df2, ignore_index=True)
   A  B
0  1  4
1  2  5
2  3  6
3  4  7
4  5  8
5  6  9
```

A more flexible way to combine objects is offered by the `pd.concat` function, which takes an arbitrary number of series, data frames, or panels as input. The default behavior resembles an append:

```
>>> pd.concat([df1, df2])
   A  B
0  1  4
1  2  5
2  3  6
0  4  7
1  5  8
2  6  9
```

The default `concat` operation appends both frames along the rows – or index, which corresponds to axis 0. To concatenate along the columns, we can pass in the axis keyword argument:

```
>>> pd.concat([df1, df2], axis=1)
   A  B  A  B
0  1  4  4  7
1  2  5  5  8
2  3  6  6  9
```

We can add keys to create a hierarchical index.

```
>>> pd.concat([df1, df2], keys=['UK', 'DE'])
      A  B
UK 0  1  4
   1  2  5
   2  3  6
DE 0  4  7
   1  5  8
   2  6  9
```

This can be useful if you want to refer back to parts of the data frame later. We use the `ix` indexer:

```
>>> df3 = pd.concat([df1, df2], keys=['UK', 'DE'])
>>> df3.ix["UK"]
   A  B
0  1  4
1  2  5
2  3  6
```

Data frames resemble database tables. It is therefore not surprising that Pandas implements SQL-like join operations on them. What is positively surprising is that these operations are highly optimized and extremely fast:

```
>>> import numpy as np
>>> df1 = pd.DataFrame({'key': ['A', 'B', 'C', 'D'],
                        'value': range(4)})
>>> df1
   key  value
0    A      0
1    B      1
2    C      2
3    D      3
>>> df2 = pd.DataFrame({'key': ['B', 'D', 'D', 'E'],
                        'value': range(10, 14)})
>>> df2
   key  value
0    B     10
1    D     11
2    D     12
3    E     13
```

If we merge on key, we get an inner join. This creates a new data frame by combining the column values of the original data frames based upon the join predicate, here the key attribute is used:

```
>>> df1.merge(df2, on='key')
   key  value_x  value_y
0    B        1       10
1    D        3       11
2    D        3       12
```

A left, right and full join can be specified by the how parameter:

```
>>> df1.merge(df2, on='key', how='left')
   key  value_x  value_y
0    A        0      NaN
1    B        1       10
2    C        2      NaN
3    D        3       11
4    D        3       12
```

```
>>> df1.merge(df2, on='key', how='right')
   key   value_x   value_y
0   B          1        10
1   D          3        11
2   D          3        12
3   E        NaN        13
>>> df1.merge(df2, on='key', how='outer')
   key   value_x   value_y
0   A          0       NaN
1   B          1        10
2   C          2       NaN
3   D          3        11
4   D          3        12
5   E        NaN        13
```

The merge methods can be specified with the how parameter. The following table shows the methods in comparison with SQL:

Merge Method	SQL Join Name	Description
left	LEFT OUTER JOIN	Use keys from the left frame only.
right	RIGHT OUTER JOIN	Use keys from the right frame only.
outer	FULL OUTER JOIN	Use a union of keys from both frames.
inner	INNER JOIN	Use an intersection of keys from both frames.

Reshaping data

We saw how to combine data frames but sometimes we have all the right data in a single data structure, but the format is impractical for certain tasks. We start again with some artificial weather data:

```
>>> df
          date      city   value
0   2000-01-03   London        6
1   2000-01-04   London        3
2   2000-01-05   London        4
3   2000-01-03   Mexico        3
4   2000-01-04   Mexico        9
5   2000-01-05   Mexico        8
6   2000-01-03   Mumbai       12
7   2000-01-04   Mumbai        9
8   2000-01-05   Mumbai        8
9   2000-01-03    Tokyo        5
10  2000-01-04    Tokyo        5
11  2000-01-05    Tokyo        6
```

If we want to calculate the maximum temperature per city, we could just group the data by city and then take the max function:

```
>>> df.groupby('city').max()
           date    value

city

London   2000-01-05      6
Mexico   2000-01-05      9
Mumbai   2000-01-05     12
Tokyo    2000-01-05      6
```

However, if we have to bring our data into form every time, we could be a little more effective, by creating a reshaped data frame first, having the dates as an index and the cities as columns.

We can create such a data frame with the pivot function. The arguments are the index (we use date), the columns (we use the cities), and the values (which are stored in the value column of the original data frame):

```
>>> pv = df.pivot("date", "city", "value")
>>> pv
city        London  Mexico  Mumbai  Tokyo
date

2000-01-03       6       3      12      5
2000-01-04       3       9       9      5
2000-01-05       4       8       8      6
```

We can use max function on this new data frame directly:

```
>>> pv.max()
city

London      6
Mexico      9
Mumbai     12
Tokyo       6
dtype: int64
```

With a more suitable shape, other operations become easier as well. For example, to find the maximum temperature per day, we can simply provide an additional axis argument:

```
>>> pv.max(axis=1)
date
2000-01-03    12
2000-01-04     9
2000-01-05     8
dtype: int64
```

Data aggregation

As a final topic, we will look at ways to get a condensed view of data with aggregations. Pandas comes with a lot of aggregation functions built-in. We already saw the describe function in *Chapter 3, Data Analysis with Pandas.* This works on parts of the data as well. We start with some artificial data again, containing measurements about the number of sunshine hours per city and date:

```
>>> df.head()
    country      city        date  hours
0   Germany   Hamburg  2015-06-01      8
1   Germany   Hamburg  2015-06-02     10
2   Germany   Hamburg  2015-06-03      9
3   Germany   Hamburg  2015-06-04      7
4   Germany   Hamburg  2015-06-05      3
```

To view a summary per city, we use the describe function on the grouped data set:

```
>>> df.groupby("city").describe()
                      hours
city
```

```
Berlin       count   10.000000
             mean     6.000000
             std      3.741657
             min      0.000000
             25%      4.000000
             50%      6.000000
             75%      9.750000
             max     10.000000
Birmingham count   10.000000
             mean     5.100000
             std      2.078995
             min      2.000000
             25%      4.000000
             50%      5.500000
             75%      6.750000
             max      8.000000
```

On certain data sets, it can be useful to group by more than one attribute. We can get an overview about the sunny hours per country and date by passing in two column names:

```
>>> df.groupby(["country", "date"]).describe()
                              hours
country date
France   2015-06-01 count   5.000000
                    mean    6.200000
                    std     1.095445
                    min     5.000000
                    25%     5.000000
                    50%     7.000000
                    75%     7.000000
                    max     7.000000
         2015-06-02 count   5.000000
                    mean    3.600000
                    std     3.577709
                    min     0.000000
                    25%     0.000000
                    50%     4.000000
                    75%     6.000000
                    max     8.000000
UK       2015-06-07 std     3.872983
                    min     0.000000
                    25%     2.000000
                    50%     6.000000
                    75%     8.000000
                    max     9.000000
```

We can compute single statistics as well:

```
>>> df.groupby("city").mean()
            hours

city
Berlin          6.0
Birmingham      5.1
Bordeax         4.7
Edinburgh       7.5
Frankfurt       5.8
Glasgow         4.8
Hamburg         5.5
Leipzig         5.0
London          4.8
Lyon            5.0
Manchester      5.2
Marseille       6.2
Munich          6.6
Nice            3.9
Paris           6.3
```

Finally, we can define any function to be applied on the groups with the `agg` method. The above could have been written in terms of `agg` like this:

```
>>> df.groupby("city").agg(np.mean)
hours

city

Berlin          6.0
Birmingham      5.1
Bordeax         4.7
Edinburgh       7.5
Frankfurt       5.8
Glasgow         4.8
...
```

But arbitrary functions are possible. As a last example, we define a `custom` function, which takes an input of a series object and computes the difference between the smallest and the largest element:

```
>>> df.groupby("city").agg(lambda s: abs(min(s) - max(s)))
        hours
```

```
city
Berlin          10
Birmingham       6
Bordeax         10
Edinburgh        8
Frankfurt        9
Glasgow         10
Hamburg         10
Leipzig          9
London          10
Lyon             8
Manchester      10
Marseille       10
Munich           9
Nice            10
Paris            9
```

Grouping data

One typical workflow during data exploration looks as follows:

- You find a criterion that you want to use to group your data. Maybe you have GDP data for every country along with the continent and you would like to ask questions about the continents. These questions usually lead to some function applications- you might want to compute the mean GDP per continent. Finally, you want to store this data for further processing in a new data structure.

- We use a simpler example here. Imagine some fictional weather data about the number of sunny hours per day and city:

```
>>> df
         date      city   value
0    2000-01-03   London     6
1    2000-01-04   London     3
2    2000-01-05   London     4
3    2000-01-03   Mexico     3
4    2000-01-04   Mexico     9
5    2000-01-05   Mexico     8
6    2000-01-03   Mumbai    12
7    2000-01-04   Mumbai     9
8    2000-01-05   Mumbai     8
9    2000-01-03    Tokyo     5
10   2000-01-04    Tokyo     5
11   2000-01-05    Tokyo     6
```

- The `groups` attributes return a dictionary containing the unique groups and the corresponding values as axis labels:

```
>>> df.groupby("city").groups

{'London': [0, 1, 2],
 'Mexico': [3, 4, 5],
 'Mumbai': [6, 7, 8],
 'Tokyo': [9, 10, 11]}
```

- Although the result of a `groupby` is a GroupBy object, not a DataFrame, we can use the usual indexing notation to refer to columns:

```
>>> grouped = df.groupby(["city", "value"])

>>> grouped["value"].max()

city

London     6
Mexico     9
Mumbai    12
Tokyo      6
Name: value, dtype: int64

>>> grouped["value"].sum()
city
London    13
Mexico    20
Mumbai    29
Tokyo     16
Name: value, dtype: int64
```

- We see that, according to our data set, Mumbai seems to be a sunny city. An alternative – and more verbose – way to achieve the above would be:

```
>>> df['value'].groupby(df['city']).sum()

city

London    13
Mexico    20
Mumbai    29
Tokyo     16
Name: value, dtype: int64
```

Summary

In this chapter we have looked at ways to manipulate data frames, from cleaning and filtering, to grouping, aggregation, and reshaping. Pandas makes a lot of the common operations very easy and more complex operations, such as pivoting or grouping by multiple attributes, can often be expressed as one-liners as well. Cleaning and preparing data is an essential part of data exploration and analysis.

The next chapter explains a brief of machine learning algorithms that is applying data analysis result to make decisions or build helpful products.

Practice exercises

Exercise 1: Cleaning: In the section about filtering, we used the Europe Brent Crude Oil Spot Price, which can be found as an Excel document on the internet. Take this Excel spreadsheet and try to convert it into a CSV document that is ready to be imported with Pandas.

Hint: There are many ways to do this. We used a small tool called xls2csv.py and we were able to load the resulting CSV file with a helper method:

```
import datetime
import pandas as pd
def convert_date(s):
    parts = s.replace("(", "").replace(")", "").split(",")
    if len(parts) < 6:
        return datetime.date(1970, 1, 1)
    return datetime.datetime(*[int(p) for p in parts])
df = pd.read_csv("RBRTEd.csv", sep=',', names=["date", "price"],
converters={"date": convert_date}).dropna()
```

Take a data set that is important for your work – or if you do not have any at hand, a data set that interests you and that is available online. Ask one or two questions about the data in advance. Then use cleaning, filtering, grouping, and plotting techniques to answer your question.

8
Machine Learning Models with scikit-learn

In the previous chapter, we saw how to perform data munging, data aggregation, and grouping. In this chapter, we will see the working of different scikit-learn modules for different models in brief, data representation in scikit-learn, understand supervised and unsupervised learning using an example, and measure prediction performance.

An overview of machine learning models

Machine learning is a subfield of artificial intelligence that explores how machines can learn from data to analyze structures, help with decisions, and make predictions. In 1959, Arthur Samuel defined machine learning as the, "Field of study that gives computers the ability to learn without being explicitly programmed."

A wide range of applications employ machine learning methods, such as spam filtering, optical character recognition, computer vision, speech recognition, credit approval, search engines, and recommendation systems.

One important driver for machine learning is the fact that data is generated at an increasing pace across all sectors; be it web traffic, texts or images, and sensor data or scientific datasets. The larger amounts of data give rise to many new challenges in storage and processing systems. On the other hand, many learning algorithms will yield better results with more data to learn from. The field has received a lot of attention in recent years due to significant performance increases in various hard tasks, such as speech recognition or object detection in images. Understanding large amounts of data without the help of intelligent algorithms seems unpromising.

A learning problem typically uses a set of samples (usually denoted with an N or n) to build a model, which is then validated and used to predict the properties of unseen data.

Each sample might consist of single or multiple values. In the context of machine learning, the properties of data are called features.

Machine learning can be arranged by the nature of the input data:

- Supervised learning
- Unsupervised learning

In supervised learning, the input data (typically denoted with x) is associated with a target label (y), whereas in unsupervised learning, we only have unlabeled input data.

Supervised learning can be further broken down into the following problems:

- Classification problems
- Regression problems

Classification problems have a fixed set of target labels, classes, or categories, while regression problems have one or more continuous output variables. Classifying e-mail messages as spam or not spam is a classification task with two target labels. Predicting house prices — given the data about houses, such as size, age, and nitric oxides concentration — is a regression task, since the price is continuous.

Unsupervised learning deals with datasets that do not carry labels. A typical case is clustering or automatic classification. The goal is to group similar items together. What similarity means will depend on the context, and there are many similarity metrics that can be employed in such a task.

The scikit-learn modules for different models

The scikit-learn library is organized into submodules. Each submodule contains algorithms and helper methods for a certain class of machine learning models and approaches.

Here is a sample of those submodules, including some example models:

Submodule	Description	Example models
cluster	This is the unsupervised clustering	KMeans and Ward
decomposition	This is the dimensionality reduction	PCA and NMF
ensemble	This involves ensemble-based methods	AdaBoostClassifier, AdaBoostRegressor, RandomForestClassifier, RandomForestRegressor
lda	This stands for latent discriminant analysis	LDA
linear_model	This is the generalized linear model	LinearRegression, LogisticRegression, Lasso and Perceptron
mixture	This is the mixture model	GMM and VBGMM
naive_bayes	This involves supervised learning based on Bayes' theorem	BaseNB and BernoulliNB, GaussianNB
neighbors	These are k-nearest neighbors	KNeighborsClassifier, KNeighborsRegressor, LSHForest
neural_network	This involves models based on neural networks	BernoulliRBM
tree	decision trees	DecisionTreeClassifier, DecisionTreeRegressor

While these approaches are diverse, a scikit-learn library abstracts away a lot of differences by exposing a regular interface to most of these algorithms. All of the example algorithms listed in the table implement a `fit` method, and most of them implement predict as well. These methods represent two phases in machine learning. First, the model is trained on the existing data with the `fit` method. Once trained, it is possible to use the model to predict the class or value of unseen data with predict. We will see both the methods at work in the next sections.

The scikit-learn library is part of the PyData ecosystem. Its codebase has seen steady growth over the past six years, and with over hundred contributors, it is one of the most active and popular among the scikit toolkits.

Data representation in scikit-learn

In contrast to the heterogeneous domains and applications of machine learning, the data representation in scikit-learn is less diverse, and the basic format that many algorithms expect is straightforward—a matrix of samples and features.

The underlying data structure is a `numpy` and the `ndarray`. Each row in the matrix corresponds to one sample and each column to the value of one feature.

There is something like `Hello World` in the world of machine learning datasets as well; for example, the Iris dataset whose origins date back to 1936. With the standard installation of scikit-learn, you already have access to a couple of datasets, including Iris that consists of 150 samples, each consisting of four measurements taken from three different Iris flower species:

```
>>> import numpy as np
>>> from sklearn import datasets
>>> iris = datasets.load_iris()
```

The dataset is packaged as a bunch, which is only a thin wrapper around a dictionary:

```
>>> type(iris)
sklearn.datasets.base.Bunch
>>> iris.keys()
['target_names', 'data', 'target', 'DESCR', 'feature_names']
```

Under the `data` key, we can find the matrix of samples and features, and can confirm its shape:

```
>>> type(iris.data)
numpy.ndarray
>>> iris.data.shape
(150, 4)
```

Each entry in the `data` matrix has been labeled, and these labels can be looked up in the `target` attribute:

```
>>> type(iris.target)
numpy.ndarray
>>> iris.target.shape
(150,)
```

```
>>> iris.target[:10]
array([0, 0, 0, 0, 0, 0, 0, 0, 0, 0])
>>> np.unique(iris.target)
array([0, 1, 2])
```

The target names are encoded. We can look up the corresponding names in the `target_names` attribute:

```
>>> iris.target_names
>>> array(['setosa', 'versicolor', 'virginica'], dtype='|S10')
```

This is the basic anatomy of many datasets, such as example data, target values, and target names.

What are the features of a single entry in this dataset?:

```
>>> iris.data[0]
array([ 5.1,   3.5,   1.4,   0.2])
```

The four features are the measurements taken of real flowers: their sepal length and width, and petal length and width. Three different species have been examined: the **Iris-Setosa, Iris-Versicolour,** and **Iris-Virginica**.

Machine learning tries to answer the following question: can we predict the species of the flower, given only the measurements of its sepal and petal length?

In the next section, we will see how to answer this question with scikit-learn.

Besides the data about flowers, there are a few other datasets included in the scikit-learn distribution, as follows:

- The Boston House Prices dataset (506 samples and 13 attributes)
- The Optical Recognition of Handwritten Digits dataset (5620 samples and 64 attributes)
- The Iris Plants Database (150 samples and 4 attributes)
- The Linnerud dataset (30 samples and 3 attributes)

A few datasets are not included, but they can easily be fetched on demand (as these are usually a bit bigger). Among these datasets, you can find a real estate dataset and a news corpus:

```
>>> ds = datasets.fetch_california_housing()
downloading Cal. housing from http://lib.stat.cmu.edu/modules.php?op=...
>>> ds.data.shape
```

```
(20640, 8)
>>> ds = datasets.fetch_20newsgroups()
>>> len(ds.data)
11314
>>> ds.data[0][:50]
u"From: lerxst@wam.umd.edu (where's my thing)\nSubjec"
>>> sum([len([w for w in sample.split()]) for sample in ds.data])
3252437
```

These datasets are a great way to get started with the scikit-learn library, and they will also help you to test your own algorithms. Finally, scikit-learn includes functions (prefixed with `datasets.make_`) to create artificial datasets as well.

If you work with your own datasets, you will have to bring them in a shape that scikit-learn expects, which can be a task of its own. Tools such as Pandas make this task much easier, and Pandas DataFrames can be exported to `numpy.ndarray` easily with the `as_matrix()` method on DataFrame.

Supervised learning – classification and regression

In this section, we will show short examples for both classification and regression.

Classification problems are pervasive: document categorization, fraud detection, market segmentation in business intelligence, and protein function prediction in bioinformatics.

While it might be possible for hand-craft rules to assign a category or label to new data, it is faster to use algorithms to learn and generalize from the existing data.

We will continue with the Iris dataset. Before we apply a learning algorithm, we want to get an intuition of the data by looking at some values and plots.

All measurements share the same dimension, which helps to visualize the variance in various boxplots:

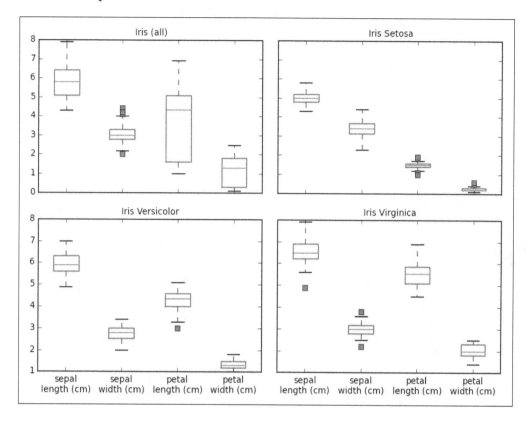

We see that the petal length (the third feature) exhibits the biggest variance, which could indicate the importance of this feature during classification. It is also insightful to plot the data points in two dimensions, using one feature for each axis. Also, indeed, our previous observation reinforced that the petal length might be a good indicator to tell apart the various species. The Iris setosa also seems to be more easily separable than the other two species:

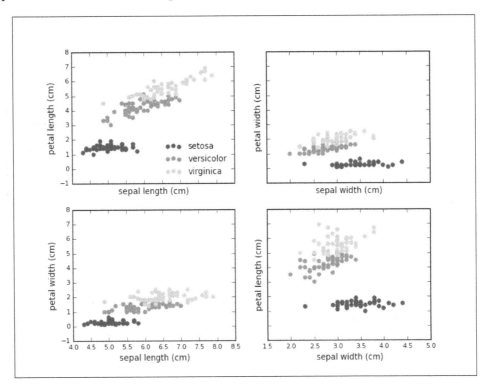

From the visualizations, we get an intuition of the solution to our problem. We will use a supervised method called a **Support Vector Machine** (**SVM**) to learn about a classifier for the Iris data. The API separates models and data, therefore, the first step is to instantiate the model. In this case, we pass an optional keyword parameter to be able to query the model for probabilities later:

```
>>> from sklearn.svm import SVC
>>> clf = SVC(probability=True)
```

The next step is to fit the model according to our training data:

```
>>> clf.fit(iris.data, iris.target)
SVC(C=1.0, cache_size=200, class_weight=None, coef0=0.0,
```

```
    degree=3, gamma=0.0, kernel='rbf', max_iter=-1,
    probability=True, random_state=None, shrinking=True,
    tol=0.001, verbose=False)
```

With this one line, we have trained our first machine learning model on a dataset. This model can now be used to predict the species of unknown data. If given some measurement that we have never seen before, we can use the predict method on the model:

```
>>> unseen = [6.0, 2.0, 3.0, 2.0]
>>> clf.predict(unseen)
array([1])
>>> iris.target_names[clf.predict(unseen)]
array(['versicolor'],
      dtype='|S10')
```

We see that the classifier has given the versicolor label to the measurement. If we visualize the unknown point in our plots, we see that this seems like a sensible prediction:

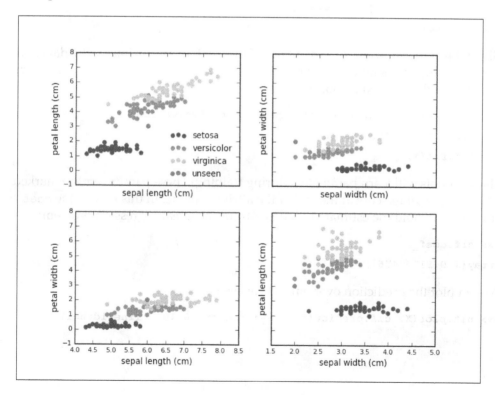

In fact, the classifier is relatively sure about this label, which we can inquire into by using the `predict_proba` method on the classifier:

```
>>> clf.predict_proba(unseen)
array([[ 0.03314121,  0.90920125,  0.05765754]])
```

Our example consisted of four features, but many problems deal with higher-dimensional datasets and many algorithms work fine on these datasets as well.

We want to show another algorithm for supervised learning problems: linear regression. In linear regression, we try to predict one or more continuous output variables, called regress ands, given a D-dimensional input vector. Regression means that the output is continuous. It is called linear since the output will be modeled with a linear function of the parameters.

We first create a sample dataset as follows:

```
>>> import matplotlib.pyplot as plt
>>> X = [[1], [2], [3], [4], [5], [6], [7], [8]]
>>> y = [1, 2.5, 3.5, 4.8, 3.9, 5.5, 7, 8]
>>> plt.scatter(X, y, c='0.25')
>>> plt.show()
```

Given this data, we want to learn a linear function that approximates the data and minimizes the prediction error, which is defined as the sum of squares between the observed and predicted responses:

```
>>> from sklearn.linear_model import LinearRegression
>>> clf = LinearRegression()
>>> clf.fit(X, y)
```

Many models will learn parameters during training. These parameters are marked with a single underscore at the end of the attribute name. In this model, the `coef_` attribute will hold the estimated coefficients for the linear regression problem:

```
>>> clf.coef_
array([ 0.91190476])
```

We can plot the prediction over our data as well:

```
>>> plt.plot(X, clf.predict(X), '--', color='0.10', linewidth=1)
```

The output of the plot is as follows:

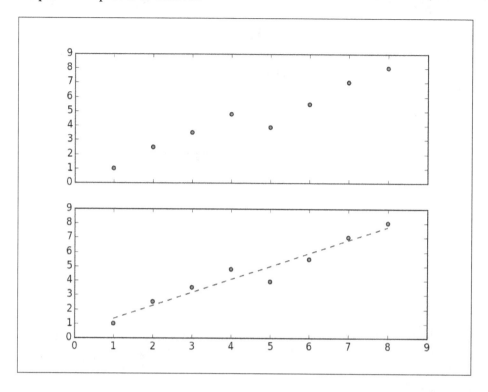

The above graph is a simple example with artificial data, but linear regression has a wide range of applications. If given the characteristics of real estate objects, we can learn to predict prices. If given the features of the galaxies, such as size, color, or brightness, it is possible to predict their distance. If given the data about household income and education level of parents, we can say something about the grades of their children.

There are numerous applications of linear regression everywhere, where one or more independent variables might be connected to one or more dependent variables.

Unsupervised learning – clustering and dimensionality reduction

A lot of existing data is not labeled. It is still possible to learn from data without labels with unsupervised models. A typical task during exploratory data analysis is to find related items or clusters. We can imagine the Iris dataset, but without the labels:

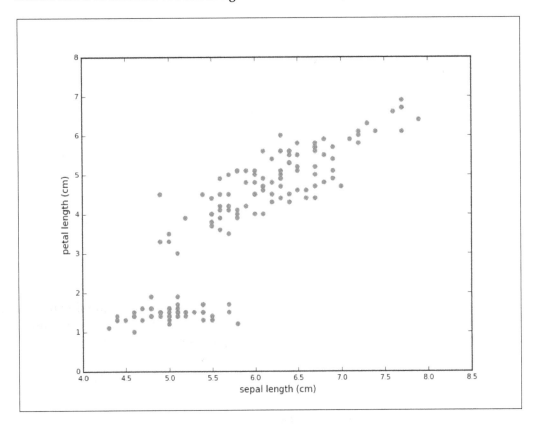

While the task seems much harder without labels, one group of measurements (in the lower-left) seems to stand apart. The goal of clustering algorithms is to identify these groups.

We will use K-Means clustering on the Iris dataset (without the labels). This algorithm expects the number of clusters to be specified in advance, which can be a disadvantage. K-Means will try to partition the dataset into groups, by minimizing the within-cluster sum of squares.

For example, we instantiate the `KMeans` model with `n_clusters` equal to 3:

```
>>> from sklearn.cluster import KMeans
>>> km = KMeans(n_clusters=3)
```

Similar to supervised algorithms, we can use the `fit` methods to train the model, but we only pass the data and not target labels:

```
>>> km.fit(iris.data)
KMeans(copy_x=True, init='k-means++', max_iter=300, n_clusters=3,
n_init=10, n_jobs=1, precompute_distances='auto', random_state=None,
tol=0.0001, verbose=0)
```

We already saw attributes ending with an underscore. In this case, the algorithm assigned a label to the training data, which can be inspected with the `labels_` attribute:

```
>>> km.labels_
array([1, 1, 1, 1, 1, 1, ..., 0, 2, 0, 0, 2], dtype=int32)
```

We can already compare the result of these algorithms with our known target labels:

```
>>> iris.target
array([0, 0, 0, 0, 0, 0, ..., 2, 2, 2, 2, 2])
```

We quickly `relabel` the result to simplify the prediction error calculation:

```
>>> tr = {1: 0, 2: 1, 0: 2}
>>> predicted_labels = np.array([tr[i] for i in km.labels_])
>>> sum([p == t for (p, t) in zip(predicted_labels, iris.target)])
134
```

From 150 samples, K-Mean assigned the correct label to 134 samples, which is an accuracy of about 90 percent. The following plot shows the points of the algorithm predicted correctly in grey and the mislabeled points in red:

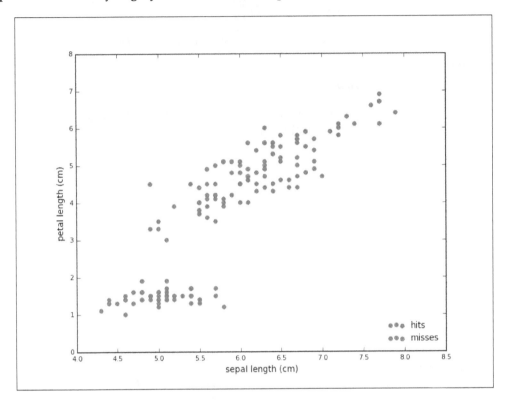

As another example for an unsupervised algorithm, we will take a look at **Principal Component Analysis (PCA)**. The PCA aims to find the directions of the maximum variance in high-dimensional data. One goal is to reduce the number of dimensions by projecting a higher-dimensional space onto a lower-dimensional subspace while keeping most of the information.

The problem appears in various fields. You have collected many samples and each sample consists of hundreds or thousands of features. Not all the properties of the phenomenon at hand will be equally important. In our Iris dataset, we saw that the petal length alone seemed to be a good discriminator of the various species. PCA aims to find principal components that explain most of the variation in the data. If we sort our components accordingly (technically, we sort the eigenvectors of the covariance matrix by eigenvalue), we can keep the ones that explain most of the data and ignore the remaining ones, thereby reducing the dimensionality of the data.

It is simple to run PCA with scikit-learn. We will not go into the implementation details, but instead try to give you an intuition of PCA by running it on the Iris dataset, in order to give you yet another angle.

The process is similar to the ones we implemented so far. First, we instantiate our model; this time, the PCA from the decomposition submodule. We also import a standardization method, called `StandardScaler`, that will remove the mean from our data and scale to the unit variance. This step is a common requirement for many machine learning algorithms:

```
>>> from sklearn.decomposition import PCA
>>> from sklearn.preprocessing import StandardScaler
```

First, we instantiate our model with a parameter (which specifies the number of dimensions to reduce to), standardize our input, and run the `fit_transform` function that will take care of the mechanics of PCA:

```
>>> pca = PCA(n_components=2)
>>> X = StandardScaler().fit_transform(iris.data)
>>> Y = pca.fit_transform(X)
```

The result is a dimensionality reduction in the Iris dataset from four (sepal and petal width and length) to two dimensions. It is important to note that this projection is not onto the two existing dimensions, so our new dataset does not consist of, for example, only petal length and width. Instead, the two new dimensions will represent a mixture of the existing features.

The following scatter plot shows the transformed dataset; from a glance at the plot, it looks like we still kept the essence of our dataset, even though we halved the number of dimensions:

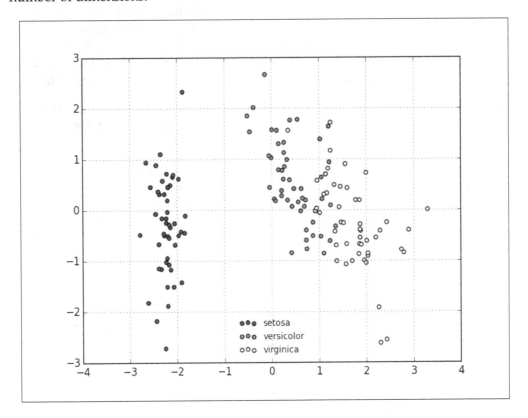

Dimensionality reduction is just one way to deal with high-dimensional datasets, which are sometimes effected by the so called **curse of dimensionality**.

Measuring prediction performance

We have already seen that the machine learning process consists of the following steps:

- **Model selection**: We first select a suitable model for our data. Do we have labels? How many samples are available? Is the data separable? How many dimensions do we have? As this step is nontrivial, the choice will depend on the actual problem. As of Fall 2015, the scikit-learn documentation contains a much appreciated flowchart called *choosing the right estimator*. It is short, but very informative and worth taking a closer look at.

- **Training**: We have to bring the model and data together, and this usually happens in the fit methods of the models in scikit-learn.

- **Application**: Once we have trained our model, we are able to make predictions about the unseen data.

So far, we omitted an important step that takes place between the training and application: the model testing and validation. In this step, we want to evaluate how well our model has learned.

One goal of learning, and machine learning in particular, is generalization. The question of whether a limited set of observations is enough to make statements about any possible observation is a deeper theoretical question, which is answered in dedicated resources on machine learning.

Whether or not a model generalizes well can also be tested. However, it is important that the training and the test input are separate. The situation where a model performs well on a training input but fails on an unseen test input is called **overfitting**, and this is not uncommon.

The basic approach is to split the available data into a training and test set, and scikit-learn helps to create this split with the `train_test_split` function.

We go back to the Iris dataset and perform SVC again. This time we will evaluate the performance of the algorithm on a training set. We set aside 40 percent of the data for testing:

```
>>> from sklearn.cross_validation import train_test_split
>>> X_train, X_test, y_train, y_test = train_test_split(
  iris.data, iris.target, test_size=0.4, random_state=0)
>>> clf = SVC()
>>> clf.fit(X_train, y_train)
```

The score function returns the mean accuracy of the given data and labels. We pass the test set for evaluation:

```
>>> clf.score(X_test, y_test)
0.9499999999999996
```

The model seems to perform well, with about 94 percent accuracy on unseen data. We can now start to tweak model parameters (also called hyper parameters) to increase prediction performance. This cycle would bring back the problem of overfitting. One solution is to split the input data into three sets: one for training, validation, and testing. The iterative model of hyper-parameters tuning would take place between the training and the validation set, while the final evaluation would be done on the test set. Splitting the dataset into three reduces the number of samples we can learn from as well.

Cross-validation (CV) is a technique that does not need a validation set, but still counteracts overfitting. The dataset is split into k parts (called folds). For each fold, the model is trained on k-1 folds and tested on the remaining folds. The accuracy is taken as the average over the folds.

We will show a five-fold cross-validation on the Iris dataset, using SVC again:

```
>>> from sklearn.cross_validation import cross_val_score
>>> clf = SVC()
>>> scores = cross_val_score(clf, iris.data, iris.target, cv=5)
>>> scores
array([ 0.96666667,  1.    ,  0.96666667,  0.96666667,  1.    ])
>>> scores.mean()
0.98000000000000009
```

There are various strategies implemented by different classes to split the dataset for cross-validation: KFold, StratifiedKFold, LeaveOneOut, LeavePOut, LeaveOneLabelOut, LeavePLableOut, ShuffleSplit, StratifiedShuffleSplit, and PredefinedSplit.

Model verification is an important step and it is necessary for the development of robust machine learning solutions.

Summary

In this chapter, we took a whirlwind tour through one of the most popular Python machine learning libraries: scikit-learn. We saw what kind of data this library expects. Real-world data will seldom be ready to be fed into an estimator right away. With powerful libraries, such as Numpy and, especially, Pandas, you already saw how data can be retrieved, combined, and brought into shape. Visualization libraries, such as matplotlib, help along the way to get an intuition of the datasets, problems, and solutions.

During this chapter, we looked at a canonical dataset, the Iris dataset. We also looked at it from various angles: as a problem in supervised and unsupervised learning and as an example for model verification.

In total, we have looked at four different algorithms: the Support Vector Machine, Linear Regression, K-Means clustering, and Principal Component Analysis. Each of these alone is worth exploring, and we barely scratched the surface, although we were able to implement all the algorithms with only a few lines of Python.

There are numerous ways in which you can take your knowledge of the data analysis process further. Hundreds of books have been published on machine learning, so we only want to highlight a few here: *Building Machine Learning Systems with Python* by *Richert* and *Coelho*, will go much deeper into scikit-learn as we couldn't in this chapter. *Learning from Data* by *Abu-Mostafa, Magdon-Ismail*, and *Lin*, is a great resource for a solid theoretical foundation of learning problems in general.

The most interesting applications will be found in your own field. However, if you would like to get some inspiration, we recommend that you look at the `www.kaggle.com` website that runs predictive modeling and analytics competitions, which are both fun and insightful.

Practice exercises

Are the following problems supervised or unsupervised? Regression or classification problems?:

- Recognizing coins inside a vending machine
- Recognizing handwritten digits
- If given a number of facts about people and economy, we want to estimate consumer spending
- If given the data about geography, politics, and historical events, we want to predict when and where a human right violation will eventually take place
- If given the sounds of whales and their species, we want to label yet unlabeled whale sound recordings

Look up one of the first machine learning models and algorithms: the perceptron. Try the perceptron on the Iris dataset and estimate the accuracy of the model. How does the perceptron compare to the SVC from this chapter?

Index

A

advanced Panda use cases
  for data analysis 52
  hierarchical indexing 52-54
  panel data 54-56
annotations 73-75
array creation 14
array functions 19, 20
artificial intelligence (AI) 2

B

bar plot 69
Berkeley Vision and Learning Center
      (BVLC) 6
Bokeh
  about 79
  differences, with matplotlib 79
  plots, creating with 79

C

Caffe
  about 6
  reference 6
computational tools 47-49
contour plot 70
cross-validation (CV) 162
csvkit tool 127

D

data
  about 1
  grouping 142, 143
  indexing 46

  selecting 46, 47
data aggregation 139-141
data analysis
  about 2
  algorithms 5
  artificial intelligence 3
  computer science 3
  data cleaning 4
  data collection 4
  data processing 4
  data product 5
  data requirements 4
  domain knowledge 3
  exploratory data analysis 4
  knowledge domain 3
  libraries 5
  machine learning 3
  mathematics 3
  modeling 5
  process 2
  Python libraries 7
  statistics 3
  steps 4, 5
DataFrame 36, 37
data, in binary format
  HDF5 112, 113
  interacting with 111
data, in MongoDB
  interacting with 113-117
data, in Redis
  interacting with 118
  list 119
  ordered set 121
  set 120, 121
  simple value 118

data, in text format
  interacting with 105
  reading 105-109
  writing 110
data munging
  about 126, 127
  data, cleaning 128-130
  data, merging 134-137
  data, reshaping 137, 138
  filtering 131-133
data processing, using arrays
  about 21
  data, loading 23
  data, saving 22
data structure, Pandas
  about 32
  DataFrame 34-37
  Series 32, 33
data types 12-14
date and time objects
  working with 84-91

E

equal (eq) function 41
essential functionalities
  about 38
  binary operations 40, 41
  functional statistics 41-43
  function application 43
  head and tail 39
  labels, altering 38
  labels, reindexing 38
  sorting 44, 45

F

fancy indexing 17
FASTLab 6
features 146
functional statistics 41-43
functions
  plotting, with Pandas 76-78
Fundamental Algorithmic and Statistical
    Tools Laboratory. *See* **FASTLab**

G

greater equal (ge) function 41
greater than (gt) function 41

H

histogram plot 72

I

interpolation 92
Iris-Setosa 149
Iris-Versicolour 149
Iris-Virginica 149

J

jq tool 127

L

legends 73-75
less equal (le) function 41
less than (lt) function 41
libraries, for data processing
  Mirador 7
  Modular toolkit for data processing
      (MDP) 7
  Natural language processing toolkit
      (NLTK) 7
  Orange 7
  RapidMiner 7
  Statsmodels 7
  Theano 7
libraries, implemented in C++
  Caffe 6
  MLpack 6
  MultiBoost 6
  Vowpal Wabbit 6
libraries, in data analysis
  Mahout 6
  Mallet 6
  overview 5
  Spark 6
  Weka 5

linear algebra
  about 24
  with NumPy 24, 25

M

machine learning (ML) 2
machine learning models
  defining 145, 146
  supervised learning 146
  unsupervised learning 146
Mahout
  about 6
  reference 6
Mallet
  about 6
  reference 6
Matplotlib 9
Matplotlib API Primer
  about 60-62
  figures 65
  line properties 63, 64
  subplots 65-67
MayaVi 79
methods
  for manipulating documents 117
Mirador
  about 7
  reference 7
missing data
  working with 49-51
MLpack
  about 6
  reference 6
Modular toolkit for data processing (MDP)
  about 7
  reference 7
MultiBoost 6

N

Natural language processing toolkit
    (NLTK) 7
not equal (ne) function 41
NumPy
  about 8, 11
  linear algebra, defining with 24

random numbers 25-28
NumPy arrays
  about 12
  array creation 14
  data type 12-14
  fancy indexing 17
  indexing 16
  numerical operations on arrays 18
  slicing 16

O

Orange
  about 7
  reference 7
overfitting 161

P

Pandas
  about 8
  data structure 32
  package overview 31
  parsing functions 109
Pandas objects
  parameters 108
PEP8
  about 12
  URL 12
plot types
  bar plot 69
  contour plot 70
  exploring 68
  histogram plot 72
  scatter plot 68
prediction performance
  measuring 160-162
Principal Component Analysis (PCA) 158
PyMongo 9
Python data visualization tools
  about 78
  Bokeh 79
  MayaVi 79, 80
Python libraries, in data analysis
  about 7
  Matplotlib 9
  NumPy 8

Pandas 8
PyMongo 9
scikit-learn library 9

Q

q tool 127

R

RapidMiner
about 7
reference 7

S

scatter plot 68
scikit-learn library 9
scikit-learn modules
data representation, defining 148-150
defining, for different models 146, 147
Series 32, 33
Single Instruction Multiple Data (SIMD) 11
Spark
about 6
reference 6
supervised learning
about 150-155
classification 150-155
classification problems 146
regression 150-155
regression problems 146
Support Vector Machine (SVM) 152

T

text method 75
Theano 7
Timedeltas 98
time series
plotting 99-102
reference, Pandas documentation 86
resampling 92
time series data
downsampling 92-94
upsampling 95, 96
time series primer 83
time zone handling 97

U

unsupervised learning
clustering 156-160
defining 156-160
dimensionality reduction 156-160

V

visualization toolkit (VTK) 79
Vowpal Wabbit
about 6
reference 6

W

Weka
about 5
reference 5

X

xmlstarlet tool 127

Thank you for buying
Getting Started with Python Data Analysis

About Packt Publishing

Packt, pronounced 'packed', published its first book, *Mastering phpMyAdmin for Effective MySQL Management*, in April 2004, and subsequently continued to specialize in publishing highly focused books on specific technologies and solutions.

Our books and publications share the experiences of your fellow IT professionals in adapting and customizing today's systems, applications, and frameworks. Our solution-based books give you the knowledge and power to customize the software and technologies you're using to get the job done. Packt books are more specific and less general than the IT books you have seen in the past. Our unique business model allows us to bring you more focused information, giving you more of what you need to know, and less of what you don't.

Packt is a modern yet unique publishing company that focuses on producing quality, cutting-edge books for communities of developers, administrators, and newbies alike. For more information, please visit our website at www.packtpub.com.

About Packt Open Source

In 2010, Packt launched two new brands, Packt Open Source and Packt Enterprise, in order to continue its focus on specialization. This book is part of the Packt Open Source brand, home to books published on software built around open source licenses, and offering information to anybody from advanced developers to budding web designers. The Open Source brand also runs Packt's Open Source Royalty Scheme, by which Packt gives a royalty to each open source project about whose software a book is sold.

Writing for Packt

We welcome all inquiries from people who are interested in authoring. Book proposals should be sent to author@packtpub.com. If your book idea is still at an early stage and you would like to discuss it first before writing a formal book proposal, then please contact us; one of our commissioning editors will get in touch with you.

We're not just looking for published authors; if you have strong technical skills but no writing experience, our experienced editors can help you develop a writing career, or simply get some additional reward for your expertise.

Python Data Science Essentials

ISBN: 978-1-78528-042-9   Paperback: 258 pages

Become an efficient data science practitioner by thoroughly understanding the key concepts of Python

1. Quickly get familiar with data science using Python.

2. Save tons of time through this reference book with all the essential tools illustrated and explained.

3. Create effective data science projects and avoid common pitfalls with the help of examples and hints dictated by experience.

Python Data Analysis

ISBN: 978-1-78355-335-8   Paperback: 348 pages

Learn how to apply powerful data analysis techniques with popular open source Python modules

1. Learn how to find, manipulate, and analyze data using Python.

2. Perform advanced, high performance linear algebra and mathematical calculations with clean and efficient Python code.

3. An easy-to-follow guide with realistic examples that are frequently used in real-world data analysis projects.

Please check **www.PacktPub.com** for information on our titles

Practical Data Analysis

ISBN: 978-1-78328-099-5   Paperback: 360 pages

Transform, model, and visualize your data through hands-on projects, developed in open source tools

1.   Explore how to analyze your data in various innovative ways and turn them into insight.

2.   Learn to use the D3.js visualization tool for exploratory data analysis.

3.   Understand how to work with graphs and social data analysis.

Learning Python Data Visualization

ISBN: 978-1-78355-333-4   Paperback: 212 pages

Master how to build dynamic HTML5-ready SVG charts using Python and the pygal library

1.   A practical guide that helps you break into the world of data visualization with Python.

2.   Understand the fundamentals of building charts in Python.

3.   Packed with easy-to-understand tutorials for developers who are new to Python or charting in Python.

Please check **www.PacktPub.com** for information on our titles